NO TIME FOR TEARS

NO TIME FOR TEARS

By Mary Shrimpton

Pine Tree Press

© Pine Tree Press
1995

Published by:
Pine Tree Press
2 Pine Tree Drive
Hucclecote, Gloucester
England

ISBN 0 9526501 0 X

Printed by

Selsey Press Ltd
84 High Street
Selsey England
PO20 0QH

Acknowledgements

The sketches of children on the cover were drawn by Julie
Williams, and are used with grateful thanks.
This book was prepared on an Acorn Risc PC, using Impression
Publisher by Computer Concepts.

Final film was prepared directly from the Acorn file by
T. J. Reproductions, London NW6 1RZ.

Contents

Introduction

Why be a foster mother? What does it entail? Many problems, hard work, dealing with dirty habits, bad language and trying to explain to small children why their own world has come crashing down around them. My world once came crashing down . . .

So many of us make plans, and I certainly made mine. The wedding first, then two years of settling down and getting accustomed to married life. Then there would be children, six of them, to be born one every two years. I was not so presumptuous as to demand what sex they should be; whatever arrived I would be satisfied.

However, my life as I planned it, went all wrong. The first two children arrived, but instead of the two years, there was three and a half. Illness had not entered into my calculations as I had always been very healthy and had not even suffered from the usual childish complaints. I had to learn a hard lesson, that it is not my plans that count, but what God has planned for me.

I certainly would not have chosen to spend a year in bed, and many months of my life receiving hospital treatment. I was to see many die, yet I was restored and so began a new life as a foster mother.

N.B. To save embarrassment, the children in this account have been given fictious names.

Chapter One

Go Home To Bed

"Go home to bed," said the doctor. I stared at her uncomprehendingly. "But I have two children and one is a baby," I argued. "How can I go to bed?"

"It's your life or the children's," she answered. "Do as I say; go to bed, and don't even lift a plate. I will visit you in a couple of days."

I left the surgery and made my way to the car. After a short while, my husband followed and we drove home in silence. Everything was perfectly normal; everything except me, and I was abnormal. I was to go to bed; I was not even to lift a plate, and all because of the pain in my chest and the blood that I had coughed up after breakfast just two weeks ago.

· · · · · · ·

It was the February of 1947. The snow lay crisp and dazzling over our small-holding. The sun shone down from a cloudless sky. It was a beautiful morning, the sort of morning that spurs the housewife on to do the tasks that have been neglected over the winter months. Spring seemed just round the corner, and by lunch-time I was very pleased with myself as I laid the table for the meal.

My elder son, Martin, who was nearly five years old, had spent the morning playing outside in the snow. Clad in an old raincoat and wellington boots, he had made a snowman, complete with hat and scarf. His younger brother, James, who was seventeen months had amused himself indoors.

After lunch we set out for our daily walk, James in his pram and Martin on his tricycle. Everywhere was white; the fields, the hedges and the boughs on the trees were hanging down with the weight of the snow. We sang as we walked, and we met no-one. We seemed to be the only ones out that afternoon. There were no people, no cars as we made a round trip from home to the next village and back along by the golf course. We were well wrapped up and the pale sunlight gave a feeling of warmth, so we arrived home hungry and tired, but very happy.

When our appetites had been satisfied and the children bathed and put to bed, my husband went to attend to the animals, shutting them down for the night. I pulled a pouffe up to the fire and sat down with pad and pen to outline a children's story I had in mind. Suddenly, without warning whatsoever, a sharp pain shot through my chest, and I found I could not breathe easily. Every breath hurt; it was like a knife being thrust into me. I staggered across the room taking shallow gasps. Indigestion, I thought. What was mother's remedy? Bicarbonate of soda. I went to the cupboard, found a small box on

2

the top shelf and promptly took a dose. The pain eased off a little so I decided on an early night, hoping that I should be better in the morning.

We were up early as was our custom. The pain had abated but it still hurt to breathe deeply. A sudden cough brought up a show of blood. I remembered that I had moved furniture in the dining- room on the previous day, so perhaps I had strained myself. A visit to the doctor seemed the wisest course to take, so we bundled the children into the car and set off. The snow plough had been before us and had cleared the centre of the road, piling it high on each side. This was the first time the children had seen so much snow and they were both very excited.

There were few patients in the surgery that morning, so I did not have to wait long before my name was called. The doctor tested my chest and said that every thing was normal, but she would send me for an X-ray because of the pain.

The result of the X-ray showed up an unusual shadow on my right lung which could have been there for many years, so I was told to come back in three weeks time and have more X-rays. A Harley Street specialist was studying my case, as it appeared that I was a very interesting one, or at least that my lung was.

Attending my own doctor to find out the results, I was told those fatal words, "Go home to bed," and my whole life was changed.

Chapter Two

Unclean

I slowly mounted the stairs, took off my clothes, and folded them up methodically, spinning out the time. Putting on my nightdress, I climbed into bed and sat up. I did not really feel ill, only very tired. The pain that I had experienced a month ago was now gone, and I felt it was the result of moving the furniture around. The piano didn't look much different on the other side of the room and I wished now that I had not bothered to move it.

No doubt I had strained myself, at least that is what I had thought until this morning. Surely doctors did not send their patients to bed for strains, forbidding them to lift a plate. No, it must be something more serious. But why had the doctor not told me. She had called my husband back as I left the surgery, so I suspected that he knew. After a short time he came upstairs and sat on the bed.

"You know what the trouble is, don't you?" he queried. Oh yes I knew. I had chewed it over as I mounted each stair, as I folded each garment and as I sat patiently waiting for him to come upstairs.

"Yes," I answered, "I know," not even wanting to say the dreaded word. He looked somewhat relieved so I ended abruptly, "I've got cancer." Now that it was out I felt better. What had to be faced must be faced in the open.

"Cancer!" he exclaimed. "You haven't got cancer. You have pulmonary tuberculosis, T.B. for short."

My spirits rose. A great weight seemed to be lifted from me, I felt reprieved. "Is that all?" I queried. Whatever was all the fuss about, going to bed, and not even to lift a plate. I only had tuberculosis, not the dreaded cancer.

How naïve I was! I should have known how serious tuberculosis could be. Our neighbours, a young couple with two small children were very friendly with us and the husband had tuberculosis. He had a wracking cough and sweated so much at night that his pyjamas and bedding had to be washed each morning. He had bought his small-holding so that he could work in the open air. They had a boy the same age as our Martin and they were inseparable, careering round the holdings in their toy pedal cars at a dangerous speed. They had moved away while I was pregnant with James and we had visited them in their new nursery. John had been very poorly and was confined to bed and then some months later he had died.

Somehow, it did not register; I did not have a cough and I certainly never sweated. I was just the opposite, always shivering with cold. So how was it that I had T.B.? If I had caught the disease from my neighbour during my pregnancy, why had I gone down with it when James was now seventeen months old?

So many questions all waiting to be answered but the most important one was how were we to manage with me in bed? The woman who had been helping me for a couple of hours each morning took fright at the mention of T.B. and fled. Her sister urgently needed her at home was the excuse. I was amazed at the number of people who were scared to come near me.

I remember particularly one morning sitting on the bottom stair and feeling utterly dejected. A smell of burning had made me leave my bed and go down to investigate. A saucepan had been left on the electric stove and the water had completely evaporated leaving burnt potatoes. Don had gone further down the small holding taking the children with him, forgetting his preparations for the mid-day meal. It must have been difficult for my husband. The outside, the inside and the children all needed attention. The tears overflowed as I cried to the Lord, "Oh Lord I feel like Job. Every one has deserted me. Please don't you leave me. Send someone to help."

God has promised, "I will never leave you nor forsake you," and "Underneath are His everlasting arms." Oh, how I needed those arms that morning! I switched off the electricity and went back to bed.

My best friend was the doctor who was very

young and new at her job but very practical. Her visits were unhurried and she took a fancy to James who was very quick to respond and held out his arms pathetically to her when she arrived. She spent time with him, nursing him and comforting him because he was so bewildered over the situation we were in. He could not understand why Mummy was always in bed.

My mother-in-law came and helped when she could, but she had a family at home who needed her. She did some cleaning and took the washing home but there were the children's daily clothes and James had nappies on at night. How I would have appreciated the disposable nappies which the mums have nowadays! A friend of mine who was a nurse came and helped with the children when she was able to fit it in with her duties at the hospital.

In sheer desperation we sought help from the large institution for the homeless, known in those days as the workhouse. They supplied us with a mother and child who had no fixed abode and the mother was very willing to come to us and for a moderate wage look after us all.

I will gloss over the following weeks. It was like living in a perpetual nightmare and sometimes I thought it would never end. The radio poured out 'pop' music from early morning until late at night. Many times when our 'help' was hanging out the washing, I would creep down and switch it off but it was soon turned on again when she was back inside. She could not work without music, not that she did much work as I would classify it; but she cooked, and at least we were fed. So were the pigs who consumed the large amount of wastage.

The children ran riot outside, and screams and shouts floated up to me through the open window. Wet or fine made no difference; the children wallowed in the puddles, and without coats they were often soaked. The outcome was that James became ill and was an added patient for the doctor who diagnosed bronchitis. She called in night and morning until he was on the mend.

One morning we had an unexpected visitor, at least *we* did not expect him but no doubt our house keeper, as she proudly called herself, did. He was her boy-friend or ex-husband, I never really knew. As he also had no fixed abode, she begged for him to stay for a few days. He had travelled down from the north to see her, and it was a very fond reunion.

A few days later Martin went down with measles and I really felt that I could bear no more. In the early hours of the morning, Don sponged the little hot body with luke warm water and his temperature dropped. There were now three patients for our busy doctor.

Our health visitor came to see me and inform me that my name had been put down for a bed in the sanatorium a few miles away. So this was the end; I would never see my children again. I was going away to die. The health visitor sat on the bed and reasoned with me.

"We wouldn't send you away if we thought

you were going to die. There aren't enough beds for everyone, so we send the ones that have a chance to get well. It sounds awful but it's true, and we have given you priority because of the children. The quicker we get you there, the quicker we will get you home." I was allocated a bed the following week.

The day before I was due to go I said goodbye to the children. My husband and his brother took James to my sister who lived about seventy miles from us. Martin went to my mother-in-law's house until he was pronounced free from infection. He would join his cousins a few miles from us. It was to be many months before we were reunited.

Chapter Three

Pick Up That Dinner

The ambulance drove up. I was sitting on the stairs, ready and waiting. The house was very quiet. The temporary housekeeper and her son had left with my husband to go back to the institution, leaving a trail of destruction behind. That very morning the small boy had found a hammer and had battered the keys on the piano from bass to treble, breaking the ends of many of them. Don and I were very upset over this, as the piano was a much-loved and appreciated possession.

Putting on my dressing gown and slippers, I went down to the door and opened it. Two ambulance men greeted me with a stretcher. Horror of horrors! I was not going on a stretcher. I could walk to the ambulance. After all, I only had T.B. and surely one did not need a stretcher for that. Stretchers were for really ill people or for those with broken legs or backs.

"You're a bed case," said one officer cheerfully. "That's why two of us have come."

I was sorry to deprive them of their prey, but I

walked to the ambulance which was parked in the drive a few yards from the front door. One officer carried my case; the other the empty stretcher. I was helped in and I sat on the seat facing the window, the stretcher having been put back in its place. This was my first experience of riding in an ambulance. I was amazed to see that I could look through the dark windows at the world outside, and yet I knew that no one could see me sitting rigidly on the end of my seat, staring out at them.

We arrived at the sanatorium, or 'san' as it was known, in time for tea, and I was allocated a bed in the pavilion. This was a long, prefabricated building with twenty four beds in it. The beds were not all facing each other as in a hospital ward, but all the beds looked out over the lawns and gardens. The long windows, from floor to ceiling, were completely open at night, exposing those on the front row to the elements. Macintoshes were provided to keep the rain from our beds, but during the winter months we often awoke to find the bottom half of the bed covered in snow.

Our water froze in our glasses overnight so we often added orange juice and then had fruit lollies in the morning. We kept our hot water bottles constantly filled, and polo necked jumpers were pulled on over pyjamas. Bedsocks were always asked for and I received many pairs made by the old ladies at our church. We boasted who had the most blankets, and at one period I was the winner with eight. This was because I had to sit up night and day, so with five pillows and all my blankets tucked around me, I surveyed the others as they were tucked in cosily for the night, some with blankets over their heads. No-one really envied me my extra blankets.

But I was to find all this out in the future. I had just arrived and my first mistake was to be wearing a nightie. Pyjamas were the thing to wear, so my first request from home was for someone to go out and buy me two pairs. Meanwhile I had to manage with a nightie, which was not very easy. The only parts of my body that the sanatorium was interested in were my lungs, and they are in the upper half. With the bottom half encased in trousers, the upper half could be exposed ready for the various needles that were constantly stuck into us.

I soon experienced my first needle. This was not to administer an antibiotic; antibiotic treatment was yet to be developed. No, the aim was to collapse one of my lungs by inserting air into the pleural cavity. Twice a week this method was used, and I queued up outside the treatment room for my refill of sterile air. For the first two weeks I felt quite ill, but then my body began to adjust.

My appetite had gone and I found that it was almost impossible to eat. I remember one particular day when the nurse put my dinner on the bed table. After giving one look at it I put the untouched plate on the locker. The nurse, who was by this time several beds down the ward, looked around and saw what I had done. Calling me by my surname, she shouted "Pick up that dinner and eat!" Feeling like a small child I removed the plate from the locker and placed it back on the table before me. I sat and looked at it very conscious of the many pairs of eyes staring at me. When everyone had been served, the nurse wheeled the trolley back down the ward and stopped at my bed.

"You really have to start eating," she said. "If you don't, there's going to be a time when you can't eat, and by the look of it that time isn't very far away."

"But it won't go down," I gulped, as the tears threatened to overflow.

"Listen," she said. "If you don't eat, you'll die. It's as simple as that. Now this is what we will do. I shall be doing the dinners all this week, and I shall give you one potato and a very small portion of whatever is going. You will eat it just to please me."

She took my plate away and returned with a very, very small portion. I took it, and because of her exceeding kindness, I managed to eat it. I could not let her down, and several weeks later when I was demanding second helpings, especially when it was kippers for breakfast, the nurse and I would laugh over her sheer brutality in showing me up in front of the whole ward.

"I had to do it," she said, "I could see you just slipping away."

Needless to say, I did not slip away, although my specialist told me that my condition had worsened considerably during the time I had been home. The X-ray showed a shadow spread over the lung, with a cavity in the middle, and I, in my ignorance, had thought that there was nothing much wrong with me.

"In three months she wouldn't have been here", he casually remarked to the nurse who was helping him in the treatment room. "She owes a big thank you to her doctor when she gets home, for the prompt attention she received."

As I lay on the treatment bed, my arm outstretched above my head waiting for the needle, I thanked God for His loving concern over me, and for giving me a caring doctor and a bed in the sanatorium, where I could receive treatment. Oh yes, I would certainly thank my doctor when I was home again.

Time passed, and I was allowed up for one hour, and then two and so on, until I was up all day. Eleven months later I at last arrived home, although not completely cured. That was to take another two years of treatment at the nearest hospital, first weekly and then fortnightly and at last monthly for refills of air.

My life had been spared, but the future was yet unknown. It was a strange feeling going back into the outside world, and trying to pick up the threads of the old life. My outlook had changed; my values had changed and I was a very different person from the one who had left home nearly a year earlier. How I used to worry over trivialities, like the breaking of a special vase or a cherished piece of china! These things did not to matter any more; I had become acquainted with death, although not many actually died in the sanatorium. Beds were needed and patients were sent home to die. News of their passing always filtered back to us. We were a close community and we all grieved.

Many months passed before we were reunited as a family. James was the last one to come home and he had to get to know his new mummy as he was now three years old. When he remarked one morning, "I think I'll stay in this house," I knew that life was returning to normal.

Chapter Four

A Visit to London

When Martin was nine years old I became very broody. I saw my friends with their new babies and I longed for one for myself. On one of my periodic visits to the specialist I broached the subject. He was not at all co-operative, and turned on me angrily, "You have two fine boys, why can't you be content?"

Content? I found it hard to be content and very hard when friends were showing off their new offspring. I had two, but there was still the question of the other four, so where were they to come from?

One evening when the boys were in bed, I picked up a newspaper and began idly turning the pages. An advertisement caught my eye. "Kindly women to become foster parents to deprived children." There followed the name of a London Borough. I read it several times before folding it and putting it away, and then finished tidying the room and going to bed.

I could not get to sleep and I thought over my life and the wonderful plans that I had made. So many things had happened that I certainly never planned for. Pain, suffering and the parting from my children for so long was an experience I would rather not have had. The six children that I wanted had not materialised and now the specialist was saying that I should have no more. I thought again of the old hymn.

"I am not skilled to understand,

What God hath willed, what God has planned."

What was God's plan for me? I did not know, and as I thought over the advertisement, I wondered if I would have the special love that would be needed to 'mother' other people's children. I did not know that night that I would have my six children, and fifty or so more in the following years.

The next morning, after the boys had gone to school, I took out the paper, and looked at the advertisement. Fetching paper and envelope, I wrote to the address given, stating details of my family. Leaving the housework and the preparations for dinner, I cycled to the post office and posted my letter.

I eagerly waited for a reply and after two weeks I had a letter. A child care officer, as they were called in those days, would be coming to see me on a given date.

Miss Jones arrived on a Monday morning. She went on a conducted tour of the house and then we settled down for a cup of coffee and chat. She needed the names of two referees, preferably local people, and I supplied her with the names of two whom I thought would vouch for me. She expressed a wish to see Martin and James who were at school, so I invited her back to tea. In the interval she was going to take up the references with which I had supplied her.

The boys arrived home, untidy and boisterous, but by the time Miss Jones rang the bell, they were spruced up. I hoped that they would be on their best behaviour, but I had no need to worry. They were marvellous, and Miss Jones went away with a very good impression, not wholly true I had to admit. She passed us as an excellent family for fostering, and said that I would be hearing from her in due course. It was decided that I should have a little girl about ten months old, and that she would match my family as much as possible in every way.

Miss Jones departed and I thought that in a couple of weeks I should have my new foster daughter, but I waited twelve months before the message came. In a large institution there was a fourteen month old girl who needed a mummy. I was asked to visit on a certain date and Miss Jones would meet me in London and accompany me. After the long wait I could hardly believe the good news. I was overjoyed and excited.

Miss Jones met me at the London terminus and together we made our way to the institution. We stood outside a massive oak door upon which was a big knocker with which we announced our arrival! The door opened and we went up a wide staircase in a building rather like a hospital. On each landing was a large window overlooking a yard filled with prams and in each pram there was a child, either sitting or lying. This depressed me and turning to the officer who was escorting us, I asked her, "Why are all those children in prams?"

"It's their rest hour," was the answer.

"But so many," I exclaimed.

"Well, there is some snag which means that they cannot be put out for fostering or adoption," she said, and we made our way to the top of the building in silence. I felt so sad to think that so many children were doomed to be institutionalised, never to know the love and sharing of family life.

We entered a small room and sat down. The child that I had come to visit was brought to me and I sat her on my lap. She had fair hair and blue eyes and could easily have been my biological daughter but she made no response as I chatted to her. I asked if she were a little backward, but the sister pounced angrily upon me and the child was taken away, back to whereever in that gaunt building she spent her time.

I looked at Miss Jones and sighed still thinking of all those children in the yards. "Cheer up," she said, "you can't take all those children you saw. Just one will help."

"Can I have time to think it over for a few days?" I asked.

"Of course," answered Miss Jones. She looked at me intently and then said, "I happen to know that there is a baby to be put out for fostering with a view to adoption. Matron doesn't like prospective mothers to see more than one child, but I can take you to see Miranda if you would like that."

I was delighted; after all it was a baby that I really wanted, so, like two naughty children, we crept down corridors, descending various staircases until we came to the baby ward. We met nobody, so there was no awkward moment when the question would be asked why we were in that part of the building.

Miranda was dark-skinned with jet black hair. She was six months old, her mother was in a mental hospital and her father had rejected her. My heart went out to her. Now I was in a quandary. Which one should I take?

We made our way out of the building and Miss Jones went back to her office, while I made my way, via the underground trains to Kings Cross. After an hours wait, I boarded a train for the long journey home.

The next few days were filled with indecision. I dearly wanted Miranda, and yet I had waited a whole year for Josephine and I really should not have seen the little dark-skinned baby. Josephine had been chosen for me; she matched my family in every way, so I would take her. I confirmed my decision and said that I would fetch her in one week's time.

Chapter Five

Just Like Me

The week passed in feverish activity. A year ago I had been ready but as the months had passed with no news of a child, I had ceased my preparations. Once again the cot was put up in the small bedroom; small dresses and other necessities were purchased, and by the end of the week I was ready.

Once again I boarded the London train, this time with a pushchair and a parcel of borrowed clothes. Once again I knocked on the massive oak door, but this time by myself. I climbed the wide staircase but purposely refrained from looking out of the windows. I went into Sister's room and waited for Josephine to be brought to me.

I sat her on my knee and talked to her before undressing her and changing her into her new clothes. Then we were ready to go. I did think that I might have been offered a cup of tea, but there seemed to be no time in that establishment for the personal touch. I picked up Josephine and the pushchair, and descended the stairs. The door was opened for me by a nursery nurse and I was let out into the busy street. We were on our own now and I wondered how the child would react to London's traffic, but everything went well.

Arriving at Kings Cross station I found that I had a long wait before my train was due to depart, so I went into the Buffet. Looking around to find a table, I noticed a middle-aged woman sitting on her own. I went over and asked if I could leave my small daughter in her pushchair by her table, while I went to the counter for coffee and milk. She agreed and when I returned we sat and chatted until it was time for us both to go to our respective trains.

I settled myself comfortably in a corner seat opposite a very stout lady who was reading a magazine. She looked up and smiled at Josephine and then asked, "What's her name?"

"Josephine," I replied.

"How old is she?" was the next question.

"Fourteen months," I answered.

Her next comment took me completely by surprise. She was staring hard at both of us then she exclaimed, "Isn't she just like you. There's no mistaking to whom she belongs."

I could not just think of an answer to this, so cuddling the child on my lap, I smiled at the lady and then looked out of the window. "Has she any brothers or sisters?" was the next question.

"She has two brothers at home," I answered truthfully.

"I guess they make a fuss of her," she said.

I wondered how the lady would react if I told her that the two brothers had never seen the little sister who was so much like me. Needless to say, I did not enlighten her.

Josephine fell asleep and for a while there was silence in our carriage. The lady went back to her magazine and I stared out of the window, watching the countryside as we passed by, and thinking over the events of the last two weeks. As we were nearing our home station, I prepared to waken the child who had slept most of the long journey. The lady also began putting her belongings together as it seemed that she was going to alight at the same station. Once again she started up a conversation. "I guess her daddy makes a fuss of her," she remarked as she lifted her case down from the rack. I was in the process of getting my things together and trying to wake up Josephine, so I refrained from answering. When my pushchair had been put by the door, she turned to me and asked "Does she cry when you wake her from a sleep?"

I had no idea whether she would or would not, whether she was one of the placid ones or one that protested vigorously when awakened. Sending up a quick prayer to my Father in heaven to take control, I answered, "She will be all right," and of course she was.

We left the train, the lady ambling behind us. Near the entrance stood Don, waiting with the car for the remaining journey of four miles. He opened his arms, and Josephine toddled into them. He swung

23

her up onto his shoulder as he used to do to the boys when they were small. The lady passed us with a satisfied look on her face.

Chapter Six

An Unexpected Visit

Jo very quickly and without fuss settled into our home and it seemed that she had always been with us. She followed the boys around learning to kick a football, and could stand up for her own rights. She was pushed high on the swing; the boys and their friends entertained her and every one around loved her. We began to think of adoption; her mother had relinquished all claim, and her father was no longer in contact.

The blow fell about seven weeks later when Miss Jones came unexpectedly in the early evening. Jo was in the bath, being prepared for bed amidst much splashing and fun. At first it seemed to be just a social call but, when the little one was tucked up in bed, Miss Jones revealed the real reason for her visit.

It had come to the notice of Jo's grandmother that her grandchild had been put out to foster with adoption in view. She had at once contacted her other daughter, who had been trying without success for the past twelve years to conceive a child and although having several operations was still infertile.

Grandma wanted this daughter to adopt Jo, and she was very willing. It all seemed very strange and confusing, but I agreed for the aunt and uncle to visit us.

They arrived a few days later, and I heard a great deal of the family background, of the quarrel that had separated the family; they had not seen Jo since she was a few days old. They played with Jo and then stayed to tea. Although I felt very angry about losing Jo, I knew that I could not fight to keep her. These people were her blood relations and had more right to her, although we loved her dearly. One thing puzzled me: I had waited for this child a whole year and had thanked God for giving her to me. Now she was to go.

At last the dreaded day arrived. It was a Saturday, so both the boys were home. Jo looked beautiful in a new pink dress and a pink bow in her hair, but she did not understand what was going on. Don said his "goodbye" and took himself off to the farthest part of the small holding which was a five acre plot. Martin stayed in the house, and was sniffing audibly; he was very upset over the parting. The car arrived and Miss Jones knocked on the door. She was alone.

"Where is Jo's auntie?" I asked.

"She is crying in the car. She is so sorry that she is doing this to you," was the answer.

"Tell her to come in. I'm the one who ought to be crying, not her," I argued.

Mrs Johnson came in, her eyes very red and

26

with a hankie held to her nose. "I'm so sorry," she sobbed. "I wish I hadn't got to do this to you."

"But yet you are doing it," I thought, "so why make all the fuss?"

Martin's sniffing became louder and I rounded on him, "Stop it! There's nothing for you to cry about. Josie is going to live with her auntie and uncle because they haven't any children." I picked up Jo, gave her a final hug and then carried her out to the waiting car. Untwining her arms from my neck, I handed her to her aunt. She began to cry loudly and turning to her aunt, I said, "You had better stop crying too, or she will be more upset." I must have sounded very brusque and unfeeling, but it was the only way I could keep myself from breaking down. We waved until they were out of sight and then went back into the house.

James, who was still swinging on the gate was sent to fetch Don to tell him that we wished to go out. It was decided that we should go swimming, so a miserable little family left the house to enjoy, or at least pretend to enjoy, an afternoon at the open air baths.

Arriving home during the early evening I was the first to enter the house. The high chair stood in its normal place; Jo's bib lay across it, and various small toys were scattered about the room. I was overcome with desolation.

Oh how I wished I had taken Miranda. She would never have matched our family with her dark skin and black hair, but what did that matter? She was a baby, and her father had gone back to his native country. We would have loved her.

We had loved Josephine and now she was gone. The boys missed her and nothing seemed the same. We were now once again a family with two boys and must be content. However, in the following weeks I lost a stone in weight.

Chapter Seven

Try Again

My doctor looked at me and shook his head, "You will never be right again until you try again," he said after examining me. My loss of weight was worrying but there seemed nothing really wrong with. He had been abroad during my illness and the female doctor had been his locum. She was now married and had left, so the practice was back to normal.

"But the same thing could happen and I couldn't go through that experience again," I answered.

"It's not likely to happen the second time," he said firmly. "Go home and think about it." I did not need to think; I knew! I just did not want my family hurt again. It was not fair on the boys.

The days passed and my longing for another child became more and more urgent. As I prayed about it I realised how presumptuous I was to want a child specially chosen for me, when there must be so many children desperate for a home. I knew then what I would do, I would find a child whom nobody wanted, and once the idea had germinated, I was eager to get going.

I did not quite know how to go about it, but nothing daunted, I travelled to our nearest large town and found the offices of the Social Services. I was shown into a room and chatted across the table to a middle-aged man who listened sympathetically as I told him of my past experience, ending up with, "So have you a baby whom nobody wants? I don't want to be matched, I just want a child who needs a mother."

He rose from the table and went to the cupboard, returning with a file. "We have a baby who was actually born in care. Her mother was only fifteen years old, and is still in care. The baby is a girl between seven and eight months old, and is in a local nursery."

"Can I go and see her?" I asked eagerly.

"We will arrange for you to visit," he answered and I returned home full of hope.

I arrived at the nursery one afternoon and watched a young nurse feeding Mary, such a scrap of a thing with straight hair that stood on end like a brush. I nursed her while I was told her history. Such a sad story. Her young mother, who herself had been brought up in an institution, had become pregnant. She had been found a place in a mother and baby hostel, but being of a very low mentality, she could not cope. The baby deteriorated and it was found that because of the time that it took to feed, the young mother was emptying half the contents of the bottle down the sink. She would lay the baby in her cot and go off to amuse herself.

Mary was transferred to a council nursery and one special nurse was allocated to her. She was beginning to put on weight, but was still very much behind for her age, and could not sit up alone. She certainly was a challenge.

At home we discussed the baby, and decided that the whole family would go and visit her the following weekend. The boys were not allowed into the nursery but as the babies were in prams in the garden, they could get acquainted with Mary.

"Can we take her home?" they asked eagerly, the younger one almost pulling her out of the pram.

My husband was not very enthusiastic. After all, this baby was very different from Jo, and we left the nursery undecided.

After much prayer it was settled that we should take Mary, but by this time an epidemic of measles had put the nursery into quarantine. We waited anxiously, but the nursery was closed again, this time because of chickenpox.

During this time of waiting I had another visit from Miss Jones, and as I had received no notification of her coming, I was somewhat surprised. She opened her file and informed me that another baby had been found with fair hair and blue eyes, just the one for me. She was sure that this time everything would work out fine.

I thanked her but then said that I had found a baby, a baby whose fifteen year old mother was feeble minded, a baby who was frail and backward. I was just waiting until the nursery was free from infection to fetch her.

She was horrified and turned on me angrily, "Think what you are taking into your home. Think of your boys."

I interrupted her before she could say more, "I have given it much thought and this is what I want to do. This baby needs a family, this baby needs love, and we as a family can give it to her."

Miss Jones could not understand. She only dealt with perfect babies, and I think she had never heard the words of Jesus, "Let the little children come to me, and do not hinder them": all children, the perfect and the imperfect.

I thank God that attitudes have changed and now the imperfect children are welcome and adopted into caring families.

On the day before Christmas Eve we had an urgent message to fetch Mary that day before the next outbreak of infection. We hurried to the nursery and collected the baby who looked very pale and listless.

The boys were delighted with their new sister. Her very frailty made her look like a little angel as she lay in her pram. It did not matter that she could not crawl; there were two eager brothers to teach her and plenty of willing hands hands to lift and encourage her to sit up as she was unable to do this by herself. We were once again a family of five.

Chapter Eight

A Lovable Delinquent

Christmas was a very happy time, and although Mary could not understand or talk part in the fun, we propped her on the settee and her large eyes followed us around.

She settled down in her new bedroom and was a very good baby. Her hair still on end like a brush, refusing all efforts we made to smooth it down. Bath-time was not a happy occasion as she was very fearful of the water. I put her on the floor to encourage her to crawl, but she remained stationary. It was several months before she could sit alone, and then she moved across the floor on her bottom, her legs flying in all directions.

It was a great source of pleasure to visit the Baby Clinic once again, and to have contact with other mothers. Mary was very much behind in her development and, although I talked to her constantly, it seemed that she was never going to communicate. Lots of love and the co-operation of a speech therapist enabled her over the years gradually to catch up.

She loved all men with horn-rimmed glasses,

and if we were in a park or travelling in a train, this often caused me embarrassment as she held out her arms to complete strangers. Our doctor was one of the horn-rimmed males, so they were great friends when I introduced her. This was also very useful when she had the measles, since she was very ill, and he had to visit her frequently. He would sit by her cot and amuse her, convinced that it was his charm that made her so attached to him, but of course it was his glasses.

The weeks passed and one day I had a visit from a probation officer based in London. My name had been given to him as a likely person to help with delinquent children. John, was a chirpy little cockney and came from a broken home. He was used to fending for himself, roaming through the streets and shops, filling his pockets with anything he fancied. After he had been caught several times, the Juvenile Court had put him in the charge of a probation officer. I was asked if he could have a holiday with us and enjoy a taste of family life. The pigs and goats on our small holding might appeal to him and the chickens would be an added bonus.

We agreed and one morning he arrived with his probation officer, very clean and smart with new trousers, shirt and pullover, which he was anxious for me to admire. He carried a small new case in his hand and on opening it, he showed me his few belongings. Two vests, two pairs of pants, two pyjamas, two shirts and a small coloured towel with flannel to match. A small yellow toothbrush, a tube of paste and a small hair brush and comb. Everything he possessed was new, and he was very proud of his few things which had evidently been supplied to him by a local authority.

He soon settled in, and wandered around the small-holding, talking incessantly to anyone who would stop and listen to him. He loved his food, and was especially pleased when, after helping to collect the eggs, he could select one for his tea. The goats, too, were a great source of enjoyment to him and he would watch them being milked with a sense of awe; his only knowledge of milk was the bottled kind. As goat's milk is extra rich and creamy, he soon began to put on weight. He drank many a glass, whisked up with chocolate powder, and of course it was sucked through a straw.

John asked many questions, and I think that he learned quite a lot during the time he spent with us. He had never seen the sea, so we decided on a day's outing to the nearest resort, a distance of about eighty miles. We set off very early on a fine sunny morning complete with picnic basket, swimsuits, and a paraphernalia of things that the boys would need on the beach.

It is hard to imagine what the sea must look like to a seven year old who had never seen it before. We deposited ourselves, and Martin and James were soon divesting themselves of their clothes. Mary was quite happy in the small pram so I turned to attend to John, only to find that he was running across the beach to the water. The tide was out, and there was a large expanse of sand so I gave chase. However, I was too late to prevent him running into the water fully clothed and with his socks and shoes still on. He whooped with delight and then, losing his balance, he sat down with a large splash.

I hauled him out, very wet and much to the amusement of the people around who were paddling. I could not be cross with him, he looked so funny, and he no clue that children took off their clothes before entering the water. I marched him back to the others and stripped him. By this time Don had erected the wind breaker, so after finding some swimming trunks for John, I pegged out his clothes to dry in the sun. Pegs were always included in our bag of sundries, also a long piece of string, which I would peg onto each side of the breaker, thus enabling me to dry towels. The string line was very useful that day! John was now equipped for splashing in the sea, and he had a wonderful day.

The holiday came to an end and we waited for the probation officer to fetch John for his return to London. He was very sad as he packed his bag and brought it downstairs, putting it near the front door. It was a lovely morning, the sun was shining and the birds were singing but the boy wandered gloomily around the small holding, saying his farewells to the animals.

The probation officer arrived. "Have you checked his case?" he asked.

"No," I replied.

"Well I think you should," he said, and he

lifted it up. "It's much heavier than when he came."

That was understandable; he had acquired many treasures during his holiday. Some had been given to him, and some he had bought. When we had visited the shops I had watched him carefully, and had explained the consequences of taking things that did not belong to him. I had formed a good relationship with him and I could see it being broken if he came in and found me going through his case.

I looked out of the window, and saw that John was in the field with the two goats, so I reluctantly took up the case. I had talked to him frequently about pilfering and hoped that my words had taken some effect. Was I to find that all my efforts had been to no avail? I was very fearful.

There was nothing in the case that was not his by rights, and at the bottom was the little black purse that I had given to him to keep his pocket money in.

"To whom does the purse belong?" asked the probation officer. "There is no purse on his list."

"I gave it to him," I answered.

"Open it," he said. Knowing how careless I was with money and how I had tried to keep my purse out of temptations way, I was very loath to comply. He picked it up and opened it, tipping out an assortment of coins and a one pound note. I could affirm that the money belong to John, and had been given to him by various members of the family.

The case was repacked and put back by the front door. Nevertheless I felt a sense of disloyalty. I was not willing to trust the words of a seven year old boy who had told me the night before that he would not steal again. I blamed the probation officer, yet deep in my heart, I wondered if I had really wanted to know what was in that case, and if I would always have had my doubts about its contents. I shall never know, but I do know that John was a most lovable delinquent.

Chapter Nine

Never Again

On November 5th 1955, we left our small-holding and moved to a neighbouring country town. On the first evening, when darkness fell, we had an enormous bonfire with all the cardboard packing cases, and the children had their fireworks. Our large Victorian house stood on the main road, and for the first few nights I was unable to sleep. After the quiet of the country, the noise of the traffic seemed unbearable.

It took a little while to settle in. Don was now away all day with his new job, and the boys could now walk to school. I concentrated on Mary who was a very slow developer, and although twenty two months old was still not walking. The day she actually took her first steps was very exciting. One of my sons held her, and the other crouched with arms outstretched, willing her to come to him. Great was their excitement when she finally obliged!

Mary was having a great deal of attention from everyone so when we were asked if we could have Sarah who was four years old, we agreed. She had been fostered with a family who had two boys, but the placement had not been satisfactory. The family were now thinking of emigrating, and did not want to take Sarah with them, so once again she was being rejected.

She came to tea one afternoon and took control of us all. "Can I make tea?" she asked.

I explained that four year olds did not make tea in my house, but she busied herself helping with the laying of the table.On her third visit she cried when it was time for her to go home, stating that she wanted to go to bed in our house. Arrangements went ahead to keep her so after several months we were a family of six.

A year later I was asked if I would foster children in need, for short periods while their mother was in hospital. This appealed to me, and after a great deal of thought and many prayers, I said that I would be willing. A few weeks later two sisters were bought to us; Betty who was nine and Jenny who was three. Their mother was going into hospital for a hysterectomy. The Childcare Officer brought them them in the evening and Betty was holding Jenny by the hand. They both seemed a little nervous and lost, but we welcomed them to our home and the three younger girls were soon playing happily together. I found some simple embroidery for Betty to do and they soon settled in.

The stay in hospital was longer in those days, and in addition to that, the children's mother seemed to develop complications. We bought some pretty cards and Betty wrote on them while Jenny added a scribble at the bottom. These were sent a various intervals to the hospital during their mother's stay. We visited, and although the children were not allowed in, they were quite happy to stand outside the ward window and wave to Mummy inside.

Their father was a bit of a problem. He had no money, or so he said. The Childcare Officer had warned me about him, but when he visited the children, bringing them sweets, yet said he had no money for the fare home, I gave him money against my better judgement.

The children stayed with us for nearly seven weeks, and they were happy and quite settled, but when mother was fully recovered after going away for a period of convalescing, the day came for the children to return to their own home. They were collected during the morning and I waved them "goodbye" from the front door. I went upstairs and stripped their beds which gave the bedroom a forlorn look. Shutting the door, I went downstairs and put the dirty washing into the washing machine. My machine had a power wringer (how I could have done with that automatic that I use now!), and as I fed the sheets through it, I felt more and more miserable. I had not really minded parting with Betty, but the younger one, Jenny, had stormed my heart. She was so small and lovable, and I would dearly loved to have kept her.

The tears began to flow mingling with the water in the washing machine, and there and then I decided that NEVER AGAIN would I take children into my home for short periods. This was not for me; I just could not bear the parting.

Chapter Ten

A Desperate Need

The door bell rang as I was putting the casserole into the oven and I went to investigate. A tall man stood on the steps and he wished me a polite "good morning." He was a Childcare Officer from our nearest town, the same officer that I had visited in my search for a baby that nobody wanted. He showed me his credentials so I asked him in and we chatted over a cup of coffee as he outlined the nature of his visit.

"The shortage of foster-mothers to take children for short periods during a time of crisis in the home is causing us grave concern. We need someone we can call on at any time and we thought that you might be willing to help us with this problem. We know that the two children who were staying with you were very happy here, and that their mother was very grateful."

"I enjoyed having the children," I answered, "but I don't want to do it again."

"Why ever not?" he queried.

"Because I felt so awful when they went, that I

decided it was 'never again' for me."

"But you will get hardened to it," he said briskly. "Think of nurses; they become less involved in their work, and you will get used to the partings. Think of the need and how you can help."

"No, never again," I reiterated.

"But think of the children who so desperately need someone to step in and care when 'Mum' is not there. You can do this. I understand that this a Christian home, and that you uphold Christian principles, so surely as a mother you must feel that this is a work meant for you."

He could see that I was wavering, and he continued, "Can I put your name down to be used in extreme emergency?"

"Allright," I capitulated. "If you need someone desperately you can call on me."

He was profuse in his thanks and shook me warmly by the hand as we parted. I went back to the kitchen with mixed feelings but with no realisation of the number of children that would pass through our home in the coming months. I also felt that because I was labelled a 'Christian mother', It had somehow been used as a sort of blackmail against me. I had not been expected to refuse.

I was 'desperately' needed that same evening at half past ten! Police had been called in to an upset in a home. Two children were involved, a boy of seven and a girl of three, and both were running around in the street. The phone rang and I was informed that the two children were on their way to me. I quickly made up two beds, and then stood looking out of the lounge window for their arrival. Considering the late hour, they were both full of energy, and incredibly dirty. After a quick bath and a hot drink, they were soon tucked up in their beds and quickly falling asleep through sheer exhaustion. We had a quiet night.

The next morning there was great excitement in our house. Two new arrivals had appeared, and my children were eager to make their acquaintance. Janie was a little apprehensive, but Carl was delighted to show off his skills. He could somersault and stand on his head, and he soon had an admiring audience. Janie played with the dolls and was quite happy as long as I was in sight.

The second night of their stay I was called upstairs by Carl, who was lying with his arms above his head. Janie was fast asleep.

"What's the matter?" I asked.

He looked at me with a troubled face and then said, "It's so quiet here. Don't you have fighting in your house?"

"Fighting?" I queried. "What sort of fighting?"

"Well", he answered, "there's fighting in our house at night and there's a lot of noise. The chairs get broken and people get thrown out. It's awful, I pull the clothes over my head to stop me hearing the shouting." He began to sob as he relived his experiences. I put my arms around him and comforted him.

"No we don't fight in our house," I said softly,

"so you've no need to pull the blankets over your head. Lie down and I will tell you a story." It was not long before his eyelids drooped so I kissed him and went downstairs. I had never thought of our house as being a quiet one, but one small boy evidently thought it was, and to him it was peace.

It was quite a joke; our quiet house! There seemed to a great deal of noise going on. In addition to my own two boys, we had two other school boys, Dick and Roger, with us during the week. This enabled them to attend our local grammar school, but then spend the weekend with their own families several miles away. They seemed to share the same enthusiasm for kicking a ball around! One afternoon I came home after speaking at a women's meeting to find a game of football being played with great gusto in the hall. Fortunately the glass in the front door remained intact, but I decided that we would have a television. All games of football would be banned indoors, except for those on the box, and for the periods before meals, and between meals and the start of homework, the boys, together with the younger children would sit quietly, and relax. This proved very effective but even so, I do not think that by any standards we were a quiet house.

Carl and Janie stayed for a month and then had to return home. Carl begged to stay and with his arms twined around my neck he sobbed, "I don't want to go back. I want to stay here."

It was heart-rending, but home he had to go. The case against the parents could not be proved, but they would be watched carefully in the future. I found it very hard parting with the children, I knew the sort of home to which they were returning and the lack of care forthcoming.

We were going on holiday the next day and, as I packed the few remaining clothes into the cases, trying to keep the tears at bay, I kept repeating to myself "No, never again, never, never. I don't want to do this, I can't cope with the emotion." How I would have loved to have taken those children with us on holiday.

Chapter Eleven

Needed Again

After a fortnight at the sea, we returned late on a Saturday evening. There was the washing to sort out for Monday, and Sunday's dinner to prepare and then bed.

On Sunday afternoon I had an emergency call — I was needed again. It concerned a young mother of only twenty two, who had a boy of two, a girl one year old and six week old twins. She lived with her husband in cramped conditions, having two rooms at the top of an old house. That Sunday morning she found she could not cope any more, so she just walked out of the house leaving her husband and children behind. The social services were called in and the babies were taken into the nursery department of a children's home. Father could look after the other two until morning, by which time he was due to go to work, so would I have the other two in the morning? So much for my 'never again'.

Mostly my children were to come in twos in the months and years following. This was because I had stated that if two children were involved, they were not to be separated, but they were to come together. My own two sons had been separated during my illness, and the elder one had suffered considerably. I felt that one child would comfort the other, just being together.

On Monday morning the children, Philip and Sue, arrived. Mother had been found by the police and she came too. She was very tearful and did not seem at all well. I promised her that I would take great care of her little ones, and urged her to get medical help.

The children stayed with us for over six months. The young parents came to see them once a fortnight on a Sunday afternoon. These occasions were pretty hectic. The little family were left on their own but I was often called in to settle the disputes. The children really played up, and neither mum nor dad could cope, so when the time for the visit was over, I think they were glad to go. The children would stand at the door and wave them off in high spirits, having thoroughly enjoyed bossing their parents about for a couple of hours.

It was decided that Philip and Sue should go home for a few days at Christmas. I remember it was a very foggy afternoon when their father came to fetch them. I had been extra busy as it was Christmas Eve, and Don's mother, his sister and a friend were staying over the holiday. I began to think that the children would be staying too, but their father eventually arrived. I handed them over laden with presents, but both clung to me apprehensively and cried. I was their one bit of security, and they were both loathe to let me go, but I disentangled them, put them on the back seat of the car, and waved them off.

Neither of the children had been toilet trained before coming to me, so during the first two or three weeks I had had wet pants in the day as well as wet beds at night. Now both used the pottie, and we rarely had an accident in the daytime, but at night they were mostly wet. It would be nice to have a break from 'wet washing' as we called it, and it would certainly help over the holiday period.

After a few days they were back. The visit had not been very successful. The children had cried each night at bedtime and even refused to go to bed.

"Do you have a light on all night for them?" asked the very worried father.

"No," I answered. "They are tucked up and left. I don't hear them until about six in the morning, when they do their best to wake the whole house up."

Father looked at me disbelievingly. "We had to keep a light on all night, and then they didn't sleep well at all." I could just imagine the antics those two engaged in. What with the excitement of Christmas and the absence of discipline, they had given their parents a rough time.

Philip and Sue were very tired and irritable, so they were put to bed early and seemed very content to snuggle down. After a story they were soon asleep, and even slept later the next morning, evidently making up for the sleep they had lost. We had a few tantrums the following days, but we all survived and they settled down again.

At last the day came when a house was allocated for the children's parents, and it was arranged that, when they had settled in, Philip and Sue should go home. Then, when their mother felt able, she could also have the twins back from the nursery in which they were still being looked after.

During the last three weeks before the children were due to go, I concentrated on preparing them for the change. We talked about it; we packed up toys and went around to various friends saying our "Goodbyes."

The day of departure arrived, and with a last hug and a kiss they were off. Once again I was left with sadness and emptiness. They were not mine, and I knew they never would be, but I still felt a sense of loss when they went. I had seen great changes in them over the past six months.

Chapter Twelve

A Permanent Addition

The time had come to add another permanent child to the family, so once again I travelled to the offices of the Social Services and made my request. A small boy needed a home. His father, a coloured serviceman, had left the country and his mother, who was wanted by the police, could not be traced. He was two years old, and was crying when I visited him in the nursery. Sitting in his cot, he looked very forlorn.

"What's the matter with him?" I asked a young student nurse.

"Oh, nothing," she replied. "He is always crying. He's a real little misery."

The 'little misery' came to visit us on several occasions. One day, when we were all out in the garden enjoying a sunny afternoon, Matron unexpectedly called in to see us. She was just passing she said, but I was tempted to think that she came to verify my statement that Adam was a different child when away from the nursery. She had to agree and decided that he was quite ready to be transferred to us.

We were now quite a large family. There was Martin, James, Mary, Sarah and now Adam. There was also Dick and Roger who lived with us all the week, in order to attend the local school, but went home for the weekend. Life at that time was very busy as I never knew when I would be needed to 'mother' in an emergency.

My parents lived about seventy miles from us, and I remember visiting them one day with the younger children. On returning home late in the evening, I found an eighteen month old boy asleep on the settee. He had been brought at seven o'clock and my husband had agreed to look after him until I arrived home. The majority of the children came in nappies, and carried a bottle of cold tea. This one was no exception!

"I've changed his nappy," announced Don, "but I couldn't find any pyjamas."

I was so tired, but with both of us working together, we soon had the younger ones in their beds. The new arrival was then washed, and pyjamas being found, was transferred to the cot. Bed was very welcome that night!

Adam settled in very well, and enjoyed having extra children to play with. The two spare beds were rarely empty, and the cot was continually in use. The children were all so different, but I remember them for the funny things they either did or said.

There was Terry, whose mother had taken an overdose. He was overjoyed at having a bed of his own. Apparently at home he shared a communal bed, and was well acquainted with the facts of life.

There was Reggie. He was three, and was constantly telling me that he was a 'good boy', and I was continually answering, "Yes, I'm sure you are." Until one Sunday. We were all hurrying to be in time for the morning service. The dinner had been put into the Rayburn to cook in our absence, and we were off. Now on a Sunday the children were responsible for seeing to their own beds, so it was not until after midday that I went into the bedrooms. Reggie was still reminding me of how good he was so I had quite a shock when I entered his room. He had emptied a bottle of blue ink onto the middle of his white counterpane and the effect was quite startling. On being questioned, he confessed that he had taken the ink, a large bottle, from one of the older boys' bedrooms. As we stood and surveyed the damage, he was still insisting, "I am a good boy, aren't I?"

Now Sunday in our house was a different day. On waking, the children would find a small surprise packet containing a few sweets or a special biscuit or some fruit. This was eaten before getting up and we could have a little extra time in bed. My own parents had done this and I can well remember the thrill of anticipating what I should get in the morning.

After breakfast we all went to the morning service, and over the years there had been an assortment of vehicles that we had all crowded into. Home to dinner, then Sunday School for those eligible, while the smaller ones played. We had a 'Sunday Box' packed with special toys, books and games. These only came out on Sundays. Many were the request to keep out one book - just to finish, or a puzzle that was incomplete. But I was ruthless. Everything was put back until next week, and so the box was very popular. New toys were added at various times and periodically, the box had a complete change over.

Sunday tea was always very special, and we made a big thing of it. In the winter, we would have it in the lounge around a log fire, and everyone was allowed three cakes to finish with. This meant a lot of preparation but I found it very worthwhile as Sundays could have been such dull days, and the children still remember with nostalgia, their 'Sunday teas.'

Chapter Thirteen

Uninvited Guests

One Saturday afternoon I had an emergency call. A pregnant woman had been taken into hospital, and there was no-one to look after her two small boys. I never discovered anything about a father but the boys with their mother lived in a prefabricated hut.

The boys were brought to me straight from home by a child care officer who had been called in. George was four and a half and he held his little eighteen month old brother tightly by the hand. They were warmly dressed but very dirty and smelly. Justin, the younger one had wet his pants and his long trousers were sodden. Their hair was long and unkempt but very curly and both had runny noses.

Over the past months I had collected small garments from various friends when their children no longer needed them, so by now I had quite an assortment. After a bath, my husband cut their hair and they looked very presentable in their clean clothes. Their own clothes were washed and ironed, then left ready for when they returned to their Mum, which would be when she returned home with the baby.

They were a very poor family but a loving one and the boys talked a lot about home and Mummy. The elder one was very protective towards the younger, and they were two of the loveliest children that I ever had. I was taught many lessons during their stay, the most important one being that, even though a family had very little of this world's wealth, love was more important. Both children were happy in the knowledge that Mum loved them. They accepted that she was ill, and were looking forward to going back to their very poor surroundings when she was better. We shopped for pretty cards of their own choice and while George very painstakingly copied my letters, Justin was happy to scribble on his. These we sent at various intervals to the hospital.

The mother had various complications and was very ill. I phoned the hospital each day and passed on the news to the boys as much as I thought they could absorb. They were very excited over the coming of the new baby. George chatted incessantly about it, but I do not think that Justin understood much of what was going on; he was quite content to be with his big brother.

The baby was born, but soon died, and I found it quite hard to explain these happenings to George. It was decided that their mother should be sent to a convalescence home to recuperate, so the boys were with me longer than at first intended. We made a real holiday of the following weeks, picnicking and going to places so that the boys would have a store of happy memories of the 'holiday' that they had spent with us.

The day came at last. Both boys were dressed in their own clothes, their faces were clean and shining with health and excitement; they were going home. We picked a large bunch of flowers from the garden for George to take home to Mummy. When the child care officer arrived, it was the same officer that had brought them. She hardly recognised them. The sadness of parting was there as I waved them off, but the joy of seeing two happy, healthy boys going home, and witnessing their excitement helped me to overcome my own feelings.

A few hours later there was a knock at the door. On opening it I found the very same officer that just taken the children. She came in as I wondered what had gone wrong.

"I felt I must come and tell you," she said. The look on that woman's face when the two boys went in – one carrying his flowers – was something I wish you could have seen. She was overjoyed as she hugged them, I wish you could have been there, and then you would have felt very rewarded for all your hard work over the past few weeks. Their mother sends a big 'thank you' for everything."

She departed and I felt a warm glow. I thanked God that night for the privilege of being able to love and care for these little ones.

It was not until I found myself continually scratching my head, that it dawn on me that George and Justin were not the only visitors that we had given house room to. I inspected all the heads and found to my horror that we were alive with unwanted guests. I was only grateful that I had found them before the nurse who periodically inspected the children's hair at school, probing with a steel needle.

Hurrying to Boots the chemist, I whispered my guilty secret over the counter. I bought a large bottle of lotion, which I was told would 'kill them off'. When I asked for a fine tooth comb, I was told very scornfully that "they are not used now days." Nevertheless I demanded one, and I received a small black comb which I then used for many years.

Everyone was doused, from the eldest to the youngest and soon everything was under control. I made a mental note that in future I would inspect the heads of new arrivals very carefully!

Chapter Fourteen

Thrown Out

The phone rang just as we were finishing tea. A young mother from a nearby village had thrown out her two small children. I could not believe that I had heard right.

"Thrown out?" I queried.

"Yes," replied the voice from the other end. "Literally thrown out, and we've nowhere to take them. Their grandmother who lives in the same village has been approached, but she refuses to take them in."

"Bring them to me," I said. I found it hard to comprehend that a mother could just discard her two children.

"It will just be for the night," the voice said. "The problem will be sorted out in the morning. Be with you in less than half an hour," and the receiver was hung up.

I hastily inspected the beds, which I now kept permanently made up. The cot would be needed so I put a couple of soft toys on the cover, and placed a teddy in one bed. I found pyjamas to fit a four year old, and night wear for his small brother. All was put into the airing cupboard to warm up.

I went downstairs and stood by the lounge window. They were not long in arriving, and as the car stopped, their screams could be heard. The car door opened and a young child care officer holding each one by the hand, dragged them to the door. She was very harassed, and as they came inside, she murmured "what ever are we going to do?" The screams were deafening and the smell of stale urine was overpowering.

"You go," I answered, "we will cope." She went very quickly, shutting the door behind her. We went into the living room and I deposited both children onto my husband's lap. The other children stopped their activities and fetched toys to amuse the newcomers while I went upstairs to sort out day clothes and run the water in the bath. Small dungarees, teeshirts, vests, pants and socks. I deposited my bundle onto the bathroom stool and returned to the living room.

The screams had stopped and when I opened the door I found both children still on Don's lap, but being entertained by the whole family. The smell of urine was even stronger now that the children were in a warm room. I suggested that we go upstairs to the bathroom, but the children were loathe to be separated from the comfortable lap and clung on desperately. The situation was ended by Don carrying the two new arrivals upstairs and my children following noisily. The bathroom was rather crowded that night - every one wanted to help - and soon two sweet smelling youngsters were sitting eating their tea-supper at the kitchen table. Meanwhile, I quickly washed out their clothes, and after spinning them, I hung them on the rack and hoisted them up to the ceiling. They would be dry by the morning as the Rayburn was always alight and the room was warm.

When the last crumb was finished, the last drop of milk had been drunk, Billy, who was the eldest, turned to me and said in a sad little voice, "Why doesn't my Mummy want us any more?"

It was heart-rending. How could I explain to a four year old? I knew nothing of the circumstances which had brought about the situation that they were now in. All I knew was that two very small children needed a roof over their heads and a bed for the night.

"Will I go home in the morning?" was the next question. I had no idea of what would happen in the morning, but I managed somehow to console him. After a cuddle and a story, they were tucked in for the night, and they slept until morning.

After the other children had gone to school, we fetched out the toys and the two boys played happily. Every little while, Billy would stop playing and ask, "Does Mummy want me today?" or "Am I going back today?".

Just after the midday meal, I had a phone message. The children would be collected at three o'clock. They were ready and dressed in their own clothes for whoever would be coming to pick them up. A much older woman than the one who had brought them arrived and she chatted to the children.

Billy put his hand in mine and looking up at me so trustingly said, "Am I going back to Mummy?" The woman looked at me and shook her head.

What could I say? I felt so inadequate. How could a mother do this to her children? I still did not know the story, nor what had led to this tragedy. I had no idea of how it would be resolved. All I knew was that our home was just a refuge for the night, and two small boys had left their mark on it as they passed through.

Chapter Fifteen

Bright Ribbons

I think one of my greatest joys was looking after West Indian children. The ones that came to me had such marvellous names that really suited them, so different from the name that we were used to. Their hair was my greatest problem, especially with the girls. They would arrive with tight plaits covering their heads. After a few days, the plaits would need redoing, so I would loosen them very carefully. The result was always the same, I was left with a mass of frizzy hair, which bounced and sprung as I attempted to restore it to its original state.

The advice given to me by well-meaning friends varied. One suggested that I should oil it, but she did not know which sort of oil should be used. My supply of oil was in the fridge, and used solely for culinary purposes, so I hesitated to use that. As I did not like the smell of olive oil, olive oil was rejected. Someone suggested brushing the hair, but after doing this, the hair stood out like a halo. Another friend suggested wetting the hair, but this seemed to be of little use, I just could not replait it.

At last I had an idea. I brought a stock of brightly coloured ribbons, and after brushing the hair, I would tie a large bow on top. I thought the effect rather good, but what their mother thought when they returned home, I never knew.

After they had been bathed, I would rub some baby lotion into their skin, which brought up a healthy-looking glow. They were always very subdued and lethargic when they arrived, possibly due to the fact that they all came from families living in one room. They were used to sitting still, sucking cold tea from a baby's bottle, or to sleeping a great deal.

They did not seem to know how to play, not having gardens of their own. Our children, however, soon taught them. They would play ball games with them, or put them into a toy car, and chase them round. The swing was a great source of enjoyment, and after a few days they became more lively and alert. I used to tell them that they were on holiday and that we had lots of treats because of this. My own family were used to having meals out in the garden, but to these little deprived ones, it was a wonderful occasion. They had many happy memories to take back with them when they returned to their cramped conditions.

Matilda was a great delight to us. We watched her as she blossomed from a little bud to a full grown flower. On a visit to a large children's park she became the centre of attention. People stopped to watch her as she fitted around like a colourful butterfly, in her bright yellow dress with a large yellow bow bobbing up and down on her head. She twirled on the grass, skipped and sang, a really happy four year old and her happiness was infectious. She had never had life so good and she was determined to make the most of it.

She sampled everything, from the swings to the roundabout, and when she could be persuaded to leave that corner of the park, we went on a boat along the lake and back. After picnicking, we ended the outing with a ride on the little train that puffed around the park. For a little girl who was used to the the confinement of living in one room, that day must have left memories which would never be erased.

We really experienced such joy at having Matilda that we were loathe to part with her, and she did not want to leave us. Eventually, the situation at her home was straightened out, and she had to go. How we missed her, but the little coloured ones came in quick succession so there was not long to brood. I loved them all, but I shall always remember Matilda.

Moses, with his little brother Aaron, came for one night only. They were so distraught and clung to each other so pathetically, that I discarded the cot and tucked them both in together into a single bed. They slept with their arms around each other and were a little happier in the morning. By the next evening, they were back in their own home, so things worked out very quickly and fortunately for them.

Chapter Sixteen

A Companion For Adam

Very early one morning we had an emergency call. A mother and father had both taken an overdose and had been rushed to the hospital, where they later recovered. There were three children, the eldest a six year old girl and two younger boys. The girl had been taken to her grandmother, and the boys were brought to me.

I was not feeling very well at the time and had several hospital appointments, so I agreed to keep them until a permanent home could be found. After a couple of weeks, a home was found for Micky, who was the youngest, and we delivered him on the way to one of my hospital appointments. He was two years old and quite an easy child to deal with.

It seemed more difficult to find a home for Roy. I had hoped that they would go together but this could not be arranged so he stayed on with us. When at last the phone rang to say that a home had been found for him, I enquired if it would be permanent and was told that he would be staying with an older woman for a short time. The thought of him going from home to home was not acceptable to me so I refused to let him go. He would stay with us until a permanent home was found.

How thankful I was that this decision had been made. A few days later I was told that the lady to whom he was going, had been found dead in bed after suffering a heart attack. This settled the matter. We would keep him and so he grew up with our family, a companion for Adam. They were very different from each other, Roy was very clean and tidy, while Adam was a dirty little urchin.

As they grew up, the differences widened. At Sunday school Adam was inattentive and fidgeted about, while Roy sat still and listened attentively. The strange thing was, that when questioned at home about the lesson, Roy knew nothing but Adam could remember it all.

When the boys went out to tea, Roy behaved perfectly but Adam always seemed to upset his drink and took too many cakes. I lectured him well before he went but it never had much effect. Roy always came home with tales of Adam's misdeeds. I always dreaded the Open Evening at school, when parents visited the school to hear first-hand how their children's work was progressing. After waiting in the long queue, I would approach the teacher when my turn came, and brace myself to hear all the bad things regarding Adam. Roy seemed to get on well with the teachers and I was glad that they were not in the same class.

One evening, the children went off to school

for a sale that was being held in aid of some good cause. They hoped to buy cheap Christmas presents, and when they returned with all their bargains, we had half an hour of great hilarity. The 'white elephant' stall had fired their imagination, and they were laden with pieces of china and bits of glass that some mother had been glad to dispose of. Adam showed me a cat vase that he had picked up for next to nothing, and it was to be my present. The others thought it quite hideous but nothing daunted, Adam told me the price, emphasizing what a bargain it was - it cost only a few coppers - and then it was duly put away, ready to be wrapped and put with the other presents. I still have it, and do sometimes use it when it brings back memories of that evening when we laughed a lot and had such fun.

When an open air swimming baths was built quite near us, the boys wanted to go swimming. They had been with the boy Covenanters to an indoor pool and, leaving the cubicles, Adam had jumped in at the deep end, a depth of about twelve feet. He just did not stop to think that he had to walk to the other end of the pool, and as he could not swim, he had to be rescued by the leader. I think he was a bit shaken by this experience and possibly had a little more respect for the water, but even so, I was not very happy about them going on their own. I dug out my old swimming suit, and decided to go with them until they became more advanced than I was. When Roy began to take his bronze and silver medals, I felt I could leave them to get on with it.

Sometimes the girls would go with them as Sarah had already gained her medals and was very keen when time permitted, but I was content to swim just for the leisure.

Chapter Seventeen

Stephen Arrives

Stephen came to us at the age of fifteen. His father, who was in the Air Force, had been stationed abroad and his mother was going to join him. Stephen was in the process of taking 'O' level examinations, so it was felt that he should stay in England, while his sister who was younger should go with her mother.

He attended the same grammar school as two of the boys, so I suppose that it from from the education authority that she heard of me. After persistent phone calls, I decided to see the mother, but I still felt uneasy. Our home was for the deprived and less fortunate children and I did not feel that he came under that category.

She arrived one afternoon with Stephen and an Educational Welfare Officer. There was no kindred spirit between us; I felt that she was hard, and very selfish and eager to push her son off. We discussed the situation over a cup of tea. I was not very happy about it, and said so. Stephen would soon be sixteen and I felt that this was an awkward age to be thrust into a large family. He came from a home with just the two children, a family with no religious beliefs.

How would he fit into our way of life? Sunday in our house was different. We attended Sunday Services and the younger ones went to Sunday School. When I mentioned this to Stephen's mother, she could see no problem.

"It will do him good to sing hymns," she commented.

"That's not the point," I answered. "He isn't used to the hustle and bustle of a large family. He will feel like a fish out of water."

"Oh he loves children," the woman continued, "and the discipline will do him good."

"I think that Stephen should have some say in this. After all he is the one who is being left behind," I argued.

The mother turned to her son. "You would like to live here, wouldn't you Stephen?" She said. Stephen nodded.

"Another thing," I went on, "he will have to share a room with the two elder boys, and he certainly isn't used to that." I seemed to be putting as many obstructions in the way as possible, creating reasons for not having him.

At last I felt the decision should be Stephen's, and that he should go home and think very carefully about it. As they left, I said to Stephen, "It's up to you to make up your own mind. You are fifteen, and should should know if you will be happy in this sort of home. Ring or write to me when you decide."

I was sure that his mother would try to influence him. She appeared eager to pack up and go. I would be the one left with an unhappy teenager.

The letter arrived two days later. Stephen would like very much to come and live with us and he had come to this decision on his own, so he joined our family.

He fitted in quite well and stayed a long time with us, much longer that I had anticipated. After taking his 'O' level examinations, he left school and took an apprenticeship with a local engineering firm. While the other boys were busy with 'A' level, and then university entrance, he was all eager to earn his living. Instead of joining his parents abroad, he stayed on with us until his parents returned to England.

He had his first real love affair and life became more serious for him. He worked hard, and spent much of his spare time with the girl. Everything was wonderful until the girl suddenly finished the relationship and I was left with the broken pieces. This was my first experience of a love sick adolescent. He would not eat and lost a considerable amount of weight. That summer he visited his parents abroad for his holiday and I guess his mother thought I had starved him over the years.

When his father was posted back to England and the family returned to a village near us, I tactfully suggested that it was time for him to return; and after they had been back some time, he finally joined them.

Chapter Eighteen

Bengie

Bengie came to us when he was three years old. His parents were unknown - he had been found as a baby, abandoned at a railway station and taken to the children's nursery. A name had been given him, as well as a birth certificate with an approximate date of birth. He was thought to be about six weeks old and as nobody knew the actual place where he was born, 'someplace in England' was recorded on his certificate.

His story with his photo was widely circulated but nobody came to claim him, so foster-parents were found for him. Everything went well until he was three, when his foster-mother had a nervous breakdown. She was unable to cope with Bengie and his violent tempers, so I was asked to take him for six weeks to give her a break. I agreed to the temporary arrangement.

He arrived one afternoon with his foster-mother and a social worker. After introductions and a tour of the house and garden, he was left with me. Tea time came and I had my first experience of his temper when he hurled his tea across the room, then kicking furniture and doors. His screams were deafening and I began to wonder what I had taken on. Still six weeks was not a very long period, I comforted myself, and no doubt we would manage.

The six weeks passed and then began a battle: the foster-mother wanted him back; the Social Services decided otherwise, and I was the one in the middle. I received distraught telephone calls from the foster-mother accusing me of holding on to Bengie when in reality I was doing all in my power to get him sent back to her.

The Social Services had decided that Bengie should be adopted, and had found a young couple who were willing. They had already two children of different nationalities and this one would make a third. They visited us one morning and Bengie, who was on his best behaviour, charmed them. It was arranged for me to take him to visit them for a few hours the following week.

The visit proved satisfactory and I was asked to take him again the following week and stay to lunch. This also passed off very well so the next time I took him in the morning and left him, promising to collect him after lunch.

The next week the social worker took him in the morning and returned him to me at tea time. He was in a tantrum and stood on the front door step, kicking the door and screaming to be let in. That evening I had a phone call from his prospective mother.

"It's not going to work," she said. "His roots are with you."

I was not told what went wrong that day, but I guess he gave vent to his temper; perhaps his dinner went across the room. He was definitely not to be allowed to go back to his original foster-parents as it was felt that they would not be able to cope for long, and so he stayed on with us.

Over the years his tempers became more controllable but never really left him and he would explode with violence over some small incident. He was a strange mixture, a charming little boy one moment and a young tyrant the next.

I remember one morning, when he was about six years old, the Police coming in response to a "999" call. I flatly denied dialling that number and said that there must have been a mistake. They were adamant and came in and checked with the exchange. The call was traced to me. The two policemen looked at me and I was made to feel really guilty, as though I had played a hoax on them. I did not know what to do to convince them that I was innocent of this serious offence. Somebody had definitely made the call from our phone, but there was only Bengie and myself in.

Bengie was playing happily on the floor with his electric racing cars. Could it have been him, when I had been outside? I suggested this to the policemen, but they scoffed at the idea. He was much too young - no - they had decided that it was positively me. I was the guilty party and, no doubt by this time, I looked it.

I insisted on questioning the small boy who was so engrossed with his race track and was apparently taking no notice of what was going on around him. I felt this was rather unusual for him. He denied touching the phone and looked the picture of innocence as he expended his charm on the two officers.

Over the years I had caught out many a culprit by tossing a sudden, swift accusation at him or her and decided to try it now. I was convinced that while I was in the garden, Bengie had made the call. We were walking to the door when I turned suddenly and looked at him. "Why did you do it, Bengie?" I accused, and swiftly, almost before he had time to think, came the answer. "Because I wanted to see what would happen."

He saw 'what happened' many times in later years when he indulged in his many pranks, but that morning he was given a 'little talk' by one of the policemen and promised never to do it again.

The police left and I made myself a strong cup of coffee.

Chapter Nineteen

Mum, You're Mum

As the years went by, the children came and went, some for a short time and others for a longer period. All were deprived in various circumstances and we welcomed them from various cultural backgrounds. As I look at their names recorded in a little book, I remember their funny little ways and their special endearments. Then Anthony arrived.

Anthony was different. He had spent the first six years of his life in a County Council Children's Nursery, then was transferred to a mental hospital until a place was available at a special school in Scotland. He was now at the school but the problem was the holidays. The other children could go home, but he had no home to go to, so where was he to go?

I received a letter with all his details and a request that I would give him a home and let him become one of the family during the holidays, which were several times a year, the longest being summer and Christmas. The letter informed me that it would not be an easy task - he was liable to break windows, to throw toys down the lavatory, thus causing drain blockages. He would hit other children and the list went on and on, ending with, "but he is very lovable." He suffered from a disease that would eventually affect all his muscles and was on medication for epileptic fits. His mental age was about four years.

This was a challenge, so we agreed to have him. Sister Janet, from the Children's Nursery, agreed to collect him from the London terminus and bring him to me. She had looked after him from babyhood and was his one stable relationship. We had just started our midday meal, because the children who came home for this, did not have a great deal of time before returning to school, which was quite near.

Anthony was very excited as the introductions were made, and he shook hands politely with us all. I was to be Auntie in this new relationship. I allotted him a place at the table and he listened to our conversation as he ate his meal with perfect manners. I was kept busy, attending to one or another, answering questions or promising to do this or that; to us it was quite a normal occasion. When the children left for school, with the usual "Bye Mum" and "Don't forget Mum" ringing in my ears, I became aware of Anthony staring at me. Suddenly he said, "You're Mum."

"Yes", I answered, "I'm Mum."

He then began to repeat, "You're Mum, you're Mum, you're Mum." As in a flash I realised that this small boy had never become acquainted with the word "Mum." His life had been ruled by "Matron" and "Sister." To him, this was quite natural, as they had given him the only love he had ever known, but now there was a new word — MUM — and he was going to use it.

Perhaps we don't realise how many times in the course of a day, our children say this well-used word. Arriving home from school, they rush into the house shouting "Mum, where are you?" and in the morning, "Mum, where is my football jersey?" or "Mum have you washed my P.E. kit?" and we are so used to this word MUM that it often fails to register. Anthony was hooked and repeated this new word for the rest of the afternoon, addressing me non-stop, until I was quite relieved when he was tucked up in bed for the night. As I left the bedroom, he called out, "You're Mum" and rather wearily I answered, "Yes, I'm Mum."

That was one of the hardest three weeks I have ever spent. A toy tractor was hurled through the bedroom window, toys were thrown down the lavatory and he was quick to hit out with his fists at the youngest member of our family. Things became so bad that I separated them for the mornings. The younger one played at a friend's house and Anthony could have my undivided attention, which of course was what he wanted. In later months, these two became great friends and played happily together.

When we visited the shops, Anthony would run behind the counter and embrace the assistant. It was all very embarrassing and if we met a mother pushing her pram, he would stop her and look into it. He was too big to have on reins; they were not made in his size. As he was very strong, it was a question of his strength against mine.

In the next garden to us was a very tall tree and one morning when my back was turned, he was out of the door, over the fence and had climbed up the tree to the top, where he sat on a branch singing his favourite tune. I did not need to go on a diet for slimming during those three weeks. I was several pounds lighter when Anthony returned to school.

As each holiday came round, I coped better and began to look forward to having Anthony at home.

Chapter Twenty

Missing

Once a year in our town we had a carnival, ending on the Saturday afternoon with a procession of colourful floats. During the week, a fair was installed in the market place and was open every evening. The roundabout whirled, the big wheel went over and over and the noise was wide-spread.

One evening the children came in from play and prepared to get ready for bed. All but one had returned; Adam was missing. His bike was in the shed so I presumed he was still in the playing field. Roy was sent to fetch him. Both boys were now eleven years old; they shared a bedroom, went to the same school but had very different interests and circle of friends.

Roy returned after scouring around on his bike, unable to find the truant. He had his supper and went to bed. As the shadows began to lengthen, I became more anxious. Perhaps he had fallen from a tree and was lying hurt in a ditch in the playing field. Don drove off to investigate but returned without the missing boy. There was no maimed body lying in the playing field; in fact the place was empty. The children had all gone home and the gate was about to be locked. He cruised around the streets but there was no sign of Adam.

At half-past ten, I rang the police and reported the missing boy. They took down full particulars and reassured me that they would ring me as soon as they had any news. That was a very long night. I sat by the window in the lounge which was at the front of the house, my eyes focussed along the road, almost willing him to come creeping home. Morning came at last and Adam had not returned. With a heavy heart I went to prepare breakfast for the other children.

Suddenly I thought of the boy's home that was at the top of our road. A large purpose-built county council home, with a Matron whom I knew slightly. She must be used to missing boys as they often seemed to be absconding and getting into trouble. I had read their stories in the local newspaper. I rang her and enquired if she had any boys missing.

Yes, she had. One very naughty boy had not returned home last evening and was still missing. This was not the first time that he had done this and she did not seem unduly worried. I told her about Adam and asked her if she thought that they might be together. She thought it very likely, as she had seen my boy with him at the fair the evening before. Adam was handing out one pound notes to his friends and they were all having a riotous time. I went to my handbag and found a considerable amount of money missing.

I replaced the telephone feeling considerably depressed. There seemed a great gulf between a Matron and a Mother. We definitely were not on the same wave-length. If only she had phoned me or called in as she passed our house on her way home, perhaps we could have averted the trouble.

The police rang to inform me that two bikes had been taken from outside of the swimming pool the previous evening, and it was thought that the boys had gone off on them. I found it very hard to concentrate that morning, with one ear continually listening for the phone and the other listening to the needs of the family.

My 'help' arrived and went as usual upstairs to the bedrooms. A bed not slept in needed an explanation, so she was soon acquainted with the facts. She was a mother whose children had now grown up and were married so she was very interested in my family. We often talked and prayed together so that morning our work routine was abandoned. It was a matter to bring before our Heavenly Father. He knew where the boys were and we could pray that He would keep Adam safe and out of trouble.

The morning passed, the children arrived home for dinner, which somehow I had prepared on time and they were eager for news of Adam. During the meal, the police rang to tell me that the boys had been found and they were now at the police station. Would I please come and collect my boy.

The children went back to school and I went in my small car to the police station. Not being very well-acquainted with such places I was very apprehensive, but found the police very helpful and kind. I was shown into a room where Adam sat alone with an officer. He was very dirty and bedraggled having spent the night sleeping under a hedge in a field. The other boy had decided to visit his father in the next town and wanted company, so they went together. Taking the bikes from outside the swimming pool, they cycled there, but the boy's father would have nothing to do with his son, so they cycled back to their own town, put the bikes under a hedge and went to sleep. The police had picked them up in the late morning as they were walking home.

On the table were the contents of Adam's pocket, including the remains of the money, which was not very much. The police officer explained how he had questioned the boy and found him very helpful and co-operative. He was very impressed with his truthful answers and felt that the boy was really sorry for what he had done. The bikes had been returned to their owners and there now remained only the question of the money.

"I'm afraid you will have to bring charges against him," said the polices officer.

"But I don't want to bring charges," I answered, He is my boy and it was my money. I would like to be allowed to deal with it in my own way."

The police officer looked rather taken aback.

He had on various occasions had to deal with Adam's companion, who was often in trouble and Matron was no stranger to him, but he could not understand me. I was a registered foster mother, so surely I should have had the same attitude as Matron to her charges. Although Adam had our surname, it was evident from his darker skin that he was not my biological son, yet I was treating him as if he were.

I tried to explain that, whether a child was biological, adopted or fostered, in our home they were all one family - one mum and dad, and all brothers and sisters.

"Please leave him to me," I begged at the end of my explanation. "Can we go home now?"

"Very well," replied the officer, and turning to Adam, he said, "You're a fortunate lad; no charges are going to be made. Mind you stay out of trouble and don't let your Mum down. Just be careful who you make friends with, I don't want to see you in this room again."

We left the police station and were soon home. Neither of us spoke on the short journey, but as we entered the house, I turned to Adam and said, "You had better get upstairs and have a bath."

He went obediently and I watched him from the hall. When he reached the top stair, I called him by name and he turned round and looked at me.

"Don't you ever do that to me again," I said and forthwith burst in to tears. Lack of sleep, combined with the strain and stress of the past hours completely overwhelmed me and I sat on the bottom stair and sobbed.

In later years, Adam told me that seeing me crying over him was something he would never forget. After a bath and a hot meal, I sent him to bed where he slept until the next morning. He was never in trouble with the police again.

Chapter Twenty One

A Danger Element

The months passed and Anthony was now a permanent resident in our home, returning to a special school in Scotland for the school terms. He always brought some gift for me that he had made, a serviette ring made with raffia, a table mat, or a picture painted with great care, and a collection of his term's work. I was always very appreciative and treasured the various gifts, knowing the hard work and concentration that must have gone into making them.

He was in his eleventh year, and it was the month of December, when he came as usual. Sister Janet always met the train from Scotland, and drove him to us, always, it seemed arriving at dinner time. He enjoyed the journey in the car with Sister Janet, and it was a tremendous help to me.

On this particular day, he rushed into the house ready for his meal, and he was soon seated at his own place at the table. I noticed that Sister Janet was very upset, so after filling Anthony's plate I went into another room to have a few private words with her. I soon found out the reason. The school which Anthony attended as a boarder refused to take him back after the holidays. He was considered a danger element to the other children. On further enquiry, I found that there had been several attacks on other children, and also that his epilepsy was worse. As a result, his drugs had been increased.

We talked the matter over, and we also received a letter from the school and all the papers regarding Anthony. He had certainly been expelled, and without any previous warning, but he he seemed quite happy and oblivious to the fact that he was not going to return to the school.

I decided that things should go on as normal until the new year. He would enjoy his holiday for four weeks, and then perhaps another school could be found for him that was nearer to us. I would watch him carefully, and if any danger arose, putting the other children at risk, I would contact the relevant authority. They would admit him to our local mental hospital, where he had spent some time before a place had been found for him at the school in Scotland.

The following week we had a dental appointment for Anthony with the school dentist at our local health centre. This was to be a routine check up, normally carried out at school by a visiting dentist, but this time arrangements had been made for me to take him. We arrived in good time and joined the other children in the waiting room. After Anthony's notes were handed over and his particulars checked, we settled down to wait. We waited and waited; I read stories to him; I showed him pictures, and still we were not called in to the dentist. The other children, some who had come in after us, were called in and when they came out, they were taken home by an elder brother or sister who had waited for them, but still we sat and waited.

The few remaining mothers commiserated with me, but when they too went home, I began to get very annoyed. I was a busy mum and I had wasted over an hour in that waiting room. My time was precious - why were we not called in?. No one seemed able to answer my question or perhaps they did not want to. At last I was informed that a male dentist from a health centre three miles away had been sent for and he would arrive in five minutes.

When he arrived and Anthony's name was called, I insisted on going in with him. He had become very restless during the long wait, and I felt that I could deal with him better than a stranger.

The resident dentist, a female, apologised to me for the long wait, while the male dentist from the neighbouring town stood at one side of the room. They both appeared nervous, especially when Anthony began investigating various objects in the room.

"Come along, Anthony," I said. "Sit in the chair." He obliged and the nurse quickly tied an apron round him. "Open your mouth wide for the dentist to look in, " I suggested, as I stood by his side and so the examination continued. I gave Anthony the orders, the dentist carried out the inspection and the nurse filled in the details on his card. His teeth were in perfect condition; he only needed a polish, and this was accomplished amidst much giggling.

At last the ordeal was over and we could go home. Anthony was reluctant to leave, wishing to be raised and lowered several times in the chair. The dentist beamed at him, telling him what a good boy he had been. She gave him a small sample of toothpaste to take home take home and he was delighted.

"I shall have it on toast for my tea," he informed her as he shook hands very politely as we left.

The male dentist was still standing at the far end of the room. Apparently after reading Anthony's notes, the resident dentist had felt unable to cope with him alone. I wondered if she had thought that he might have a fit or become obstructive and attack her, but the services of her male colleague had not been required.

We arrived home in time for tea. Beans on toast for the other children, but not for Anthony. He would have none of it, and only wanted toast on which he carefully spread some of his new toothpaste. We were all very merry at tea that night and Anthony suffered no ill effects.

Chapter Twenty Two

Anthony is Rejected

The new year had arrived; the school holidays were over; the children had returned to their lessons. A decision had to be made for Anthony. He too needed to go to school. Enquiries were made, but his records were so bad that no place could be found for him.

Within walking distance from our home was a new special school for children like Anthony. A hostel was attached and everything was very modern. They seemed to have plenty of staff and I thought that it would be ideal for him. It would be near enough to be in close contact with us and he could come home for weekends and special days during the term. I felt that this was my answer to prayer when he was summoned to be interviewed.

I took him along one morning and we were shown around. He was introduced to the head-mistress and to the matron of the hostel. We went into the playroom to meet some of the children and Anthony was allowed to stay and play. Meanwhile his future was being discussed in an adjoining room with the headmistress, matron and the mental health specialist.

Looking round, I thought what a pleasant place this was. Everything was new and bright and I felt that the problem was solved, Anthony would love it here in these pleasant surroundings. I had prayed for the right place to be available and now there was a vacancy here. I did not know what sort of impression Anthony had made with the headmistress, but I knew that the doctor would do all in his power to obtain the place because he, as I, felt it was just the place for Anthony.

I walked into the waiting room full of hope and anticipation to await the outcome of the meeting. The door opened and the mental health specialist came and sat down beside me.

"Well?" I asked. "How did the meeting go?"

"They won't take him," he answered.

"Not take him, but why?" I argued.

"They don't think that they can manage him," he replied sadly.

This was too much to take sitting down. I became quite heated. "Not manage him, with all their staff. I manage him with no staff and all the other children, too."

He put his hand on mine, comfortingly. "You are different," he said. "You are a Mum. Don't give up, we will just have to think again. Something will turn up, I'm sure. I could overrule the decision but I don't think that it would be wise."

Screams were erupting from the playroom so

we went to investigate the trouble. Anthony had gone completely out of control and was enjoying the havoc he was causing. A red-faced staff member was trying to hold on to him, but his strength was superior to hers. I called his name sharply and reprimanded him, then went over to him. He soon calmed down and order was restored.

"See what I mean," said the doctor, who had been watching this little scene. "He needs special handling, you seem to have the knack, but they haven't got it here."

We returned home. I was feeling angry and frustrated. The staff had seemed very relieved to see us go, and the doctor had promised to be in touch with me in the near future, but we were definitely back to square one. Anthony was in high spirits, he talked of going to school, and of the lovely toys he had played with that morning. What was I going to do with him now? He needed lessons and the discipline of school life.

My prayer had not been answered - Anthony was still rejected by society as a whole - surely he was no worse than the other children I had seem that morning. He had a wonderful memory that could be stimulated; he was very musical and loved to sing, always on the right notes, and he was so loving.

At the back of my mind lurked those damaging words - a danger element, considered a risk to other children - this would follow him everywhere. Only once had we been aware of this, when teased by Adam, Anthony had picked up a knife from the table and struck him. Fortunately no damage was done and we were extra watchful over him, and teasing was now banned. No other incident had occurred.

There was only one place in the house during the day where you could be sure that Anthony would not intrude. This was the upstairs toilet and he respected the privacy of that small room, both for himself and for other people. Everywhere else in the house was 'public', but this was definitely 'private'.

I went upstairs to the little room and locked the door. My tears overflowed as I prayed, "Help me to understand Your will. I felt so sure that this school was the answer from You, but it wasn't so. It was such a lovely place, it seemed so right. Help me to understand." It was not until three months later that I finally understood that God in His wisdom had prepared a better place for Anthony.

Chapter Twenty Three

The Search Continues

Three weeks passed and I heard that there was a bed available for Anthony at our nearest mental hospital about fourteen miles away. There was a school attached to the hospital which he would attend during the day. I was given the opportunity to go and look over the place, taking him with me.

It was a beautiful afternoon, cold but sunny. We arrived on time and were shown into the waiting room. A male nurse was allocated to us, for the purpose of showing us around. We visited the school and chatted with the teacher in charge. She was very impressed with all the things that Anthony said he could do, and she told him that he would be a great help to her, especially in the tying up of shoelaces. No one in the school could do this small task for themselves, so Anthony would be kept very busy. He was very pleased about this. There was no doubt that he would be the 'star' pupil, but I was not very happy about this.

Next, we visited a large hall where children were playing. The door was unlocked for our admittance and relocked when we were inside. The sight of those children was my first real introduction to a mental hospital and I was shocked. Anthony crept up to me and held my hand, I think he was a glad as I was when we were let out.

We were then shown the ward where Anthony would sleep. Two rows of beds were placed very close together, in a long narrow room. It seemed very crowded.

"What about clothes?" I asked. Anthony was very particular over bodily cleanliness and very fussy over his clothes. He would cast aside anything which had a spot or speck of dirt on it, and every morning his pyjamas were folded neatly and put under his pillow. I had noticed that the children wore an odd assortment of clothing, nothing coordinated.

"I'm sorry," answered the nurse, "all clothes are shared. It is the easiest way of laundering."

"But surely he can have his own pyjamas. He has name tags in them," I pleaded.

"No, not even his pyjamas", was the answer. "We share."

He showed me a small room fitted out with shelves. There were various baskets and I was told that one would be allocated to Anthony. I could use it to store items like pants, vest, socks shirts and pullovers, then when I came to fetch him home, he could put them on. However, on his return, they would have to be replaced into the basket. As a special concession, he would be allowed to hang his suit on a hanger at the top of his bed.

We were taken back to an office for an interview with the chief officer, then given tea with biscuits before leaving for home. I was busy with my own thought as I drove the fourteen mile journey home. Suddenly I was aroused from my reverie by a voice, "I don't want to live in that place. I want to sleep in my own bed."

It was Anthony and I realised with a feeling of panic that I had driven through the town, out into the open country and was within two miles of home, yet had no recollection of the journey. No doubt I had stopped at traffic lights, had kept to the one way system, and had taken all the appropriate turnings. Surely the Lord had watched over me during that drive. Anthony, too, had evidently been deep in thought.

We arrived home safely, and the children were eagerly waiting for us. It was tea time.

"What was it like, Anthony?" they asked.

"I don't want to live there. I want to sleep in my own bed," came the pathetic reply.

I sent him to the bathroom to wash his hands, and as he left the room, I was besieged with questions.

"How can you send him there, Mum?" they said accusingly. "Why can't we keep him here? We can help you with him here, and he needn't go to school."

"Stop it, all of you! You don't understand," I answered. No one understood. I was so miserable. I wanted to keep Anthony, but how could I? He needed to be watched every hour of the day, and I had the other children to consider. He would be well looked after at the mental hospital, and would attend their school, although I could not see any great advantage in that. His medication would be constantly checked, and there would be a watchful eye kept on him. How he would hate being locked in, the thought persisted. But I would have him for home visits and would visit him often. Surely the Lord did not expect me to do any more than this. Why, then, was I so miserable?

"Tea time," I called, and the matter was dropped.

Chapter Twenty Four

The Final Decision

The night seemed long; I could not sleep. Over and over I pondered the matter of how to keep Anthony from going to the mental hospital. I asked God to show me very definitely if it was at all possible to keep him at home. I still had a heavy heart.

The next morning I contacted my doctor, who was a Christian, and with whom we were on very friendly terms. I asked him to explain to me as fully as was possible about Anthony's condition. He was very helpful, but could not really tell me any more than what I already knew, which was that Anthony would eventually lose the use of all of his muscles. He advised me to talk to the specialist at the local hospital when we attended the following week for Anthony's periodical examination.

It was one of his 'bad' days. We arrived at the hospital and after he had undressed, the nurse took him into an adjoining room to be examined by the specialist. I sat outside with his clothes. The noise that erupted from the inner room was dreadful.

Anthony shrieked and laughed hysterically, and I presumed that he was kicking his legs about as the nurse could be heard begging him continually to keep still.

At last I could stand it no longer. I pushed open the door and went in. Anthony was kicking and squirming on the bed, enjoying the situation he was creating.

"Anthony," I said severely, "lie still. The doctor wants to examine you." He looked at me and I could see that he was not very pleased to have his entertainment curtailed.

"Do you mind if I stay", I asked the specialist.

"Please do," he answered and proceeded to prod Anthony's tummy and various other parts of his anatomy. When the examination was over, Anthony was told to get dressed and the nurse went with him. I stayed behind to have a chat.

The report was not good. He had deteriorated since his last appointment, and there seemed to be some trouble with his kidneys. His epilepsy was worse and he was on a high dose of drugs to control it. The wasting of his muscles was beginning to show, and once again I was told that he would eventually lose the use of them.

I asked about the life span of children with this disease and was told that they did not normally live to a great age, perhaps the early twenties, but no one could really predict this.

The specialist was kind and considerate, and willingly spared the time to talk with me. Over the years, I had visited him many times with another epileptic child. I told him about the mental hospital where there was a vacant bed. I told him of my feelings when I visited and how I felt that it was not the right place for Anthony.

"Do you think it would be feasible to keep him at home? Could I stimulate him enough for a school to accept him later?" I enquired.

"I can't advise you," he answered sympathetically. "No doubt you will do what you think is right. You always seem to manage, but what a task!"

"He isn't always as bad as he was today," I defended him. "He knows that he can't get away with 'playing up' when I'm around. He was enjoying his act just now; he loves an audience. He needs a Mum and a home. I can't put him into that hospital to become a cabbage like the rest of them." My mind went back to those children in the locked hall.

The specialist looked at me kindly, then shook me by the hand. I collected Anthony, and we left the hospital.

That evening the decision was made. Don and I were in perfect agreement. Anthony would remain at home with us for three months. There would be no school during that time and at the end of it, he would either be so much better that we could apply once again for a place in a special school, or he would have become worse and we would have to think again. I felt that he was not a danger to others, and Mary, who was looking for a job, agreed to help me with him for these three months.

A great weight was lifted; every one was pleased, we could all be happy again.

Chapter Twenty Five

A Place For Anthony

One Sunday dinner time as the children were leaving the table, Anthony, for no apparent reason, fell. He picked himself up, but seemed a little wobbly on his legs as he left the room.

That was the beginning. From that day he seemed to become more unsteady and would occasionally fall down. He was still very chirpy, but less noisy and he seemed to tire more easily. The muscles had begun to deteriorate in his legs and walking became difficult. He enjoyed going for rides in the car, so walks were gradually abandoned as we drove around.

One morning he climbed out of bed to go to the toilet and immediately fell. He lay on the floor, unable to get up by himself until one of the boys came to help him. This was another problem but it was soon overcome. When he wanted to get out of bed, he would shout and someone stood by, ready to help if needed. This worked well for a time.

Once downstairs, he went around holding on to the furniture, but the day soon came when he had to be helped more frequently. Finally, I found it almost impossible to get him into the car, and I could not get him out without help, and even then it was a struggle. I knew now that there would be no going to school at the end of the three months.

The days were swiftly passing. One morning he had his usual bath, but the business of getting out was particularly hazardous. He was very tall for his age, and the disease was rapidly advancing, but we finally managed with much puffing and blowing to deposit him on the bathroom stool. We were then faced with the task of getting him downstairs and settling him onto the settee.

"The time has come," I said to Mary, "for us to bring a bed downstairs for Anthony." We busied ourselves that morning and by midday a small bed had been installed in the living room and made up ready for use.

The day came when he was confined to bed, but he was not unhappy. The children were around him; he was propped up to watch television and the youngest child waited on him, fetching and carrying for him. The two spent many an hour curled up on the bed together.

The doctor visited but there was nothing that he could do. The disease would take its course, and I was reminded once again that he would lose the use of all his muscles. It was not the case for an ordinary hospital, but he could probably be admitted to the mental hospital, the very same one we had visited. When I asked for his life expectation, I was told that it could be months.

I looked at Anthony as he lay in his bed and somehow I knew: he would not be with us for months. I felt so very sure in my own mind that his life was ebbing away. We would nurse him at home amongst his familiar surroundings.

"No, don't apply for a bed," I said to the doctor. "If there is no treatment, only his drugs, we can manage at home." The doctor left with the assurance that he would call within the month, but if I needed him I would phone him.

The following weekend, all the family, except the eldest were home. Anthony was considerably weaker, and could only swallow very small amounts which I gave him at frequent intervals, feeding him with a teaspoon. When everyone had gone to the Sunday morning meeting, I sat on his bed and talked to him. He seemed far away but I felt that he could hear me, although he made no response.

"If you can hear me, Anthony, just smile, "I coaxed.

He smiled, and I said, "Shall I sing to you?"

He smiled again. I sang many of his favourites, when suddenly I remembered what he so loved to sing, and in tune too, no matter what time of the year it was.

"Silent night?" I asked, and was rewarded with a smile. He slept for the rest of the morning.

The next day I contacted the doctor who called in before lunch time. He looked at Anthony after a brief examination and said "We won't talk in terms of months now. We will talk about weeks. Can you still manage? We've left it a bit late now, but I could no doubt get him admitted as an urgent case."

The thought of Anthony going into the mental hospital, all alone to die, was too awful to contemplate. We had managed very well up to the present, my husband and the boys being a great help, especially when it came to turning him over, as he was now a dead weight. I had solved the problem of his incontinency.

"Yes, we can manage," I answered.

After the doctor had gone, I stood looking down at Anthony. "Weeks," the doctor had said. "We wont talk in terms of months, but weeks." As I gazed down at him, I knew with deep certainty that it was neither weeks nor months that we should be thinking of for Anthony, but it was days.

During the previous weeks I had applied to the Red Cross for the hire of a wheel chair. I had hoped to take Anthony out for a daily ride. That very morning it arrived, but it was too late.

That was Anthony's last day with us. Roy helped me turn him for the night and as we made him comfortable, I said to the children, "Say goodnight to Anthony. I think this will be for the last time." I felt that there were not many hours left before Anthony would arrive in his new 'home'.

Anthony slept, and Don settled down on a camp bed near him. I was persuaded to go and lie down for a short rest. I went upstairs and lay on the bed. Now I could understand many things. I knew why the school in Scotland had rejected him: just supposing he had gone back; he would have been transferred to a hospital up there, miles away from any of us. I knew too why no school could be found for him, why the new special school that I had thought to be so wonderful had refused to take him. God in His wisdom and love had better things reserved for Anthony, and I was reminded of the children's hymn I had sung, especially those lines,

"There's a home for little children,
Above the bright blue sky."

Chapter Twenty Six

No Time For Tears

Just before midnight, Anthony left us. He slipped away without a sigh. One moment he was here, the next he was gone. No struggle, no sound, his breathing just ceased. After notifying the doctor, we tenderly washed his thin body and putting on his clean pyjamas, we laid him lovingly between clean white sheets with his head resting on the pillow. Turning the top sheet back over the blanket, I smoothed the counterpane and placed his teddy bear beside him. He looked so peaceful, as though deep in sleep.

The children were asleep, and there seemed no point in waking them. I had crept up to Sarah's room and told her as soon as Anthony had gone. She had specially requested that I should do this, and she came down. This was the first occasion that death had visited our home, and we all had to deal with it. There must be no shut doors, no fear of this natural thing that had entered our house. What horrors would be conjured up, if in the morning I said, "Don't go into the living room; Anthony died last night." A child's imagination is so vivid, they would wonder for ever what was in that room.

I remembered in my own childhood going into hospital to have my tonsils removed. One morning when I awoke, I found the bed next to mine empty. A small boy had been there when I went to sleep. I knew that he was very ill because doctors and nurses had surrounded his bed, and the curtains had been drawn. I was only five years old, and although I questioned everybody, nobody would tell me where he had gone. For months I was obsessed with fear over what happens to children when they die. Oh yes - I knew he had died - and my children would be spared this. I would be truthful, and their questions on death would be answered naturally and without evasion.

We tidied the room, put away the camp bed and leaving the door open, went upstairs to bed. As I lay and thought over the past days, I was thankful, so thankful, that a small boy had not suffered. He had been surrounded by love and the knowledge that someone was always near. He had never had to experience the loneliness of a hospital bed, when the ward is quiet and the parents have gone home. What had the future held for him — NOTHING — there was no future; his brain was damaged, and his body had become useless. I could not cry; this was no time for tears.

As the dawn broke, I fell into a light sleep. When I awoke, I sat up in bed. Had Anthony really gone or had I dreamed it? Putting on my dressing gown, I went slowly down the stairs. I stood at the open door, and looked across at the bed. He looked as he had on other mornings, but as I went nearer, I could see no movement, could hear no breathing. Anthony was not there, only his body. I pulled back the curtains to let the early sunrays in and went upstairs to tell the children.

The youngest stood at the open door. "But Anthony isn't dead," he said, "He's fast asleep."

"No," I answered, "Anthony has gone to live with Jesus. It's only his body in the bed."

He thought for a moment, then walked over to the bed. Turning to me, he observed, "It doesn't matter that he hasn't a brain now." He had always accepted the fact that Anthony had a baby brain, and in his own way, he now felt happy that this no longer mattered.

I went into the kitchen to prepare breakfast as the elder children came down the stairs. I had told them that if they did not wish to go into the living room, it would not matter. They must do as they pleased. Pausing at the door as they came through the hall, each one walked on into the kitchen. I continued making toast and frying bacon when suddenly I realised that the kitchen was empty. They had gone back into the living room. I went to the door and saw them standing silently by the bed.

"Does't he look beautiful," Roy said, and the others agreed. Anthony's face, which in life had been so spotty, was now completely clear and smooth. They came out to the kitchen for breakfast -

evidently for them this was no time for tears.

Each child said his own farewell before leaving for school and when they returned Anthony's body had been taken to the Chapel of Rest. I found the undertaker to be most helpful and kind. He understood when I explained that I wanted the children to have memories of Anthony as he lay in bed that morning, so peaceful, so beautiful, and readily agreed to come for the small body while they were at school.

He came on his own, as no one else was available, and used a small white van. James, who was home from University, assisted him, and unobtrusively Anthony's body was taken from home. As I stood by the lounge window and watched the cars and pedestrians hurrying by, I saw the small white van emerge from the side of the house and filter into the traffic. Nobody knew that inside was a 'shell' containing all that remained of a little boy, who in this world had been handicapped, but in the world to come would be perfect.

There was so much to do. I seemed as though I could not sit still - I rush here, there and everywhere - washing sheets and blankets, pegging them out on the line to dry in the sunshine. The telephone was in constant use and there was much coming and going. Was there never to be a time for tears?

Two days passed and I came downstairs early, as was usual. The living room door was open and I looked in as I passed. No bed was there, no small boy needing attention. Nothing. The full realisation hit me: Anthony had gone, never to return. The floodgates were opened; now was my time for tears.

Chapter Twenty Seven

Retrospection

The funeral was over, life went on much as before, although somewhat easier. Martin, now married, was working in Africa. Sarah was a day student at a college for Further Education about twelve miles away. James had returned to University, and the boys were at local schools. Mary went to the Geriatric Hospital, which was about two miles from home, to help the old people as a nursing orderly. I remember the day she came home after assisting in the 'laying out' of an old lady. This was her first experience and as she was very attached to the 'old dears', as she called them, she was sadly affected. After several months this became almost routine, and she would remark casually, "We had two deaths this morning, so things were pretty hectic."

I sat in the garden one afternoon and closing my eyes I began to think back over the past years. Time had passed so quickly. I remember how unhappy I had felt when the first bird had left the nest. Martin was eighteen when he left home to take his place at the University of London, and with so many at home, friends told me that I would not miss him, but of course I did. One bed remained empty, one less for meals, in fact one less for everything. No more dirty rugger kit to be washed quickly because it would be needed again soon; no more Elvis coming from the bedroom. And now he was married, and teaching in Kenya, and I was a grandmother who had not seen or touched her grandson! Oh yes, I missed him. I suppose one's firstborn always has a special place in a mother's heart, although there were no favourites in our family.

I remembered the time soon after he had moved into a hall of residence, and was now responsible for his own laundering. His vests, pants and pyjamas were a most horrible colour, a dirty blue/grey. He had put all of his laundry, underwear, socks, and a shirt into the machine together regardless of colours, and something had not been colourfast. I tried bleaching and boiling the vests and pants but there was no improvement; the unique colour remained and those clothes took a long time to wear out. They always looked dirty, but I do not think that it worried Martin.

I remembered when Sarah went for her first interview for a place in the Child Care course at the College of Further Education. We went by car and I waited for her in the college until she was ready to return home. After her interview I was summoned to the room where the interview had taken place, while she went elsewhere to complete a written test. I was faced with the three interviewers; a Home Office

Official, a Senior Social Worker, and a College Lecturer, and invited politely to take a seat.

Then the questions started. Did I think that Sarah had an aptitude for dealing with children? Had I encouraged her to apply for the course as a result of my involvement with children? Was she a very tidy girl, and was she good at needlework? As the questions went on I began to feel very uncomfortable, for I was really in a dilemma. I had not expected to be interviewed and now that I was, I must speak the truth whatever the outcome. I wondered if similar questions had been put to Sarah, and if so, how she had answered. If this was God's plan for Sarah, then everything would be all right and so my answers began.

"No, I didn't think that Sarah had any special qualities needed for dealing with children. In fact I had done my best to dissuade her from applying for the course. No, she was not a very tidy girl, and wasn't much good at needle-work because of lack of interest. She enjoyed playing the piano, had many friends, and loved messing about with cooking. She was a born manager and very capable of taking control." I felt that I was ruining her chances of gaining a place on the course, but I had argued often with her about her suitability for working with children. The patience that one needs must be inexhaustible, and a sense of humour and tolerance are necessary qualifications.

I need not have worried. There was a general laugh from the other side of the table. Sarah had been asked identical questions and had answered them in a similar manner. She had spoken truthfully about her short-comings, even telling them that her mother was always grumbling about her untidy bedroom. They had encouraged her to talk about her family, and she had told them all about our home life, about the children that came in emergencies, about the biological ones, Martin and James, and the chosen ones. The panel were most impressed. She was the most mature applicant that they had interviewed so far, and I was told in confidence that she would most definitely be offered a place on the two year course. She would be notified by post in about a week's time. Later she successfully completed the course, and later became a Junior Matron at a boys preparatory school in Somerset.

Chapter Twenty Eight

Adolescence

The time came when only Bengie was at school. We moved to smaller house in a village, where a river flowed along the bottom of a very large garden. Bengie and his friends spent many hours fishing and a small boat was an added pleasure, either to row or use with a low powered engine.

It was holiday time, and Bengie came to me with a special request. His friends were going to camp out in their garden and intended having great fun. The parents had given their permission and he was invited. All he needed was his sleeping bag.

His request being granted, he went off to build the camp. I had an appointment several miles away, and did not arrive home until late afternoon. Bengie had been in, had his tea and gone again. I checked and found that his sleeping bag had gone. Wandering through the bedrooms, I noticed that something in the spare room did not look quite right. I could not put my finger on it, but it seemed to me that the beds did not look the same as usual.

I went downstairs, but the feeling nagged me. Yes, it was definitely the beds: the quilts were on the wrong way. The two beds were always made up, ready for use, but on investigating the first bed, I found that it was positively unmade! Then the realisation hit me, that my best pink blanket was missing. I hurried over to the other bed and again found that a pink blanket had gone. Surely Bengie would not have the audacity to take two good pink blankets to camp out with. I was furious.

I left the house and walked quickly to the garden where the camp was to be. Nobody was about. I knocked on the door of the house, but there was no reply. Evidently the parents were out so I went down to the garden to investigate. A shack had been constructed from an assortment of materials and I went inside. There, sure enough, were my two pink blankets, spread out on the dirt and some wet straw, evidently doing duty as carpets. I pulled them up; they were damp and dirty. Rolling them up, I returned home with them, a disillusioned, angry woman.

The blankets would have to be washed. No amount of dabbing at the mud spots could make them clean enough to be put back on the beds. They were wet and horrible, so I put one into the washing machine and switched it on. The other would have to wait until the first was finished.

At about eight o'clock, Bengie came in looking very disgruntled. "Mother, how could you?" he said reproachfully, just as though it were my fault.

No word of apology, no acknowledgement of having done anything wrong.

I was tired and angry. Washing blankets at the end of a busy day, blankets that would not normally have needed washing, was irritating and annoying. I gave Bengie a good telling off, ending with, "You know that there are grey blankets for use out of doors." Apparently, grey blankets are not in the same class as pink ones when you are building a camp. He beat a hasty retreat with a grey blanket under his arm.

He was home very early the next morning, tired and dirty. No one had been able to sleep. They had spent the night going in and out of the house collecting food. The camp had not been a great success.

As the days passed Bengie grew more and more a law unto himself. He was constantly in trouble, but of course it was never his fault. He objected to coming home before midnight, and very often it was the early hours of the morning before he would come creeping in. Many times I left the backdoor unlocked, and tired and exhausted went up to bed, only to find the next morning that he had not returned. He always had a good excuse, like missing the last bus, or that he had tried to ring me to tell me he was staying with friends, but the phone was out of order.

He was in trouble at school, and one morning we had a visit from the headmaster. He came to inform us he could put up with Bengie no longer, and that he was being expelled. The whole school had been disrupted that morning by the fire bell ringing, and they had all assembled outside. The culprit, they decided, was Bengie.

He stole a car and took four friends for a ride during school hours. Fortunately, he managed to bring the car safely back, but then his friends decided to have a go, and the car was crashed. I became so used to the police ringing the door bell that I would greet them with, "What has he done now?" Very often it was a request to fetch him from the police station.

His tempers became more violent, and at one period he was taken from an assessment centre and put into a mental hospital where he was put under sedation. When I protested, I was told that it was the only way that the staff could control him. One Sunday afternoon he escaped and rang me from a call box, shouting hysterically for us to fetch him home. However, he was caught and once again heavily drugged.

We were to have our first experience of a juvenile court, of listening to the magistrates as they decided what should be done with him. He was sent to an approved school where he charmed everybody, and when he developed chickenpox, the governor telephoned me personally to report on his condition and to chat about him. He could not understand why Bengie had acted as reported; he was so well mannered and charming. He visited him daily, relaying messages from him to me. I was told that I could ring the school at any time and I would be constantly kept in touch. I was in no doubt that Bengie had 'conned' everyone there into thinking that it was an injustice having him sent there. He excelled in acting and often talked of the day when I would see him on the television screen.

He was my last fosterchild, and caused more heartache than any of the others. I spent more hours battling in prayer for him, and my pillow was frequently wet with the tears that I wept over him. He now asserts that he has 'turned over a new leaf,' but I have heard him say it so often that I must just wait and see.

Chapter Twenty Nine

Full Circle

The years passed; educational courses were completed; jobs were begun, and then there were weddings with all the excitement and fuss. Mary and Sarah had their first experience of being bridesmaids, and then later on they too were married.

Martin and his wife spent four and a half years in Kenya, where my first two grandchildren were born. Tapes and photos came regularly, but there was a natural sorrow in not being able to enjoy the babies. There was great joy when they were once again back in this country.

Having grandchildren is one of Gods greatest blessings. To have fun and to treat the children without the responsibility of having complete control. To laugh once again at funny comments, to tell stories at bedtime, and to listen - always to listen. I am sure that Grandparents have a great role to play, alongside parents. There is a great bond between young and old.

The dressing up box, filled to overflowing with garments of all descriptions, is now in great demand.

"Can we come and stay at your house?" is a constant request, so they take turns, two at a time. If it's summer they use their fishing nets, or swim in the river. The younger children have to be continually watched, but no one has yet fallen into the water at the bottom of the garden. The boat, now much the worse for wear, has given the elder children their first experience of rowing.

Fishing nets, blow-up arm bands, and 'wellie' boots clutter up the porch. Skipping ropes and balls lie around on the lawn. Meals have to be taken out of doors, sometimes complete with table and chairs or a picnic, sitting on a blanket near the river bed.

Yes, God is good and His mercy endures for ever. Looking back over the years, I can praise him for His faithfulness, for His wonderful care, for His healing power and for a love that knows no bounds.

I am often reminded of the words that my mother would quote, when circumstances in the family were beyond her control.

"Our lives are set in a curious plan,
  Shaping them as it were for man;
  But God with better art than we,
  Shapes them for eternity."